Jesus I

Les Marsn

Jesus decoded

the first historical translation of Luke

Les Marsh

*W*ide Margin

Published in 2010 by Wide Margin,
90 Sandyleaze, Gloucester, GL2 0PX, UK

http://www.wide-margin.co.uk/

ISBN 978-0-9565943-4-1

Printed and bound in Great Britain by
Lightning Source, Milton Keynes

CONTENTS

What is a historical translation?

A literal translation of Luke is often puzzling. It tells us 'they will see the Son of Man coming on the clouds... the powers of the heavens will be shaken... to follow me you must hate your father and mother... sell all you have and give it to the poor... the Lord praised the dishonest manager.'[1]

A historical translation solves the puzzles for us. It translates the whole story. It goes through Luke's Greek text, into the life-story of first-century Hebrew-Aramaic Jews. It uncovers hidden subtext, and reveals the forces Luke's hero faced. It empowers us to read Luke's story as his first readers might have read it.

Luke himself used historical translation. Compare his translation of some words of Jesus with another writer's, Mark:

> 'When you see "the abomination of desolation" standing where it ought not, (let the reader understand)' (Mark 13.14)

> 'When you see Jerusalem besieged by armies' (Luke 21.20)

Mark has translated Jesus' words literally, and added the cryptic, 'let the reader understand.' Luke's historical translation has decoded Jesus' Aramaic-Hebrew words for his Greek readers.

Jesus said that in public he spoke in parables – code, 'so that [the establishment] may not understand.'[2] He often marked his words as in code by adding: 'Those with ears to hear, hear!'[3]

Jesus' actions too were coded, and he rapped his men for missing this. 'Do you have eyes and fail to see?'[4]

A historical translation decodes actions. It also makes a cultural translation of events – as Luke himself does:

> 'They dug through the clay roof' – a Galilean mud roof. (Mark 2.4)
>
> 'They took off some tiles' – a Greek tiled roof. (Luke 5.19)

Luke has tuned this event to his Greek readers.

Like any ancient historian, Luke edited his material into a form best suited to his reader. The historical translator must re-edit it for today. Luke's own theology could distract today's reader, so it is not – as far as possible – translated here. It can be found by reading this historical translation alongside a traditional translation.

This work is largely in debt to the current third-historical-quest.In ancient history, complete certainty eludes. The test is whether we account for all the data, and make most sense of the history. This is a matter of judgement, and no attempt to justify this work can be made here. All that can be said here is, 'This is the only show in town!'

Some examples of the historical process

- Luke's first sentence tells us what his book is about, 'the things whose fulfilment has been accomplished...' This packs into one sentence the whole Hebrew story: to translate it we must first unpack it.

- The story tells us that the job needs a son-of-David. The translation needs to show us what this means.

- Some words carry veiled content, and need background for impact. For instance, the cold chill 'Herod' evokes, or the joy of 'resurrection' raised by Jesus saying, 'get up!'

- Some names are omitted to avoid misunder-standing or for ease of reading.

- Parts are cut where the thread might get lost, or are too slow for the modern reader.

- Luke assumes his reader knows the events of CE 70. As a climax of the story, today they need to be spelt out.

Translator's introduction

'Truth is stranger than fiction,' they say. If so, the true story of Jesus of Nazareth must be the strangest story of all. When it was first told, it set the world on fire. It was too hot for rulers and emperors to hold. People caught with it were fed to lions. The establishment said that it 'turned the world upside down.'

Historians have now unearthed the society Jesus lived in, and *Luke* fits well into that scene. It is the first professional history of Jesus – based on the evidence of eye-witnesses. It is a unique story of an ordinary man, with a humanity not found elsewhere. In a time of turbulent events, he set out to save his generation from hell-on-earth.

A historical translation reveals that human story. We think of 'translation' as 'translated words'. But historical translation translates *what is implied in the words*. It is not tied to literalism, but unfolds what the original is really saying.

The story is universally magnetic. All of us may find ourselves siding with this man. So please, don't let any so-called 'miracles' spoil the story for you. They are a red-herring. They don't affect our view of him as a man. Even his enemies thought they saw these things happen. So each of us must make of them what we will.

Forget anything you know about this man. Throw your mind back into the mindset of a young Jew two thousand years ago. Read this as you would the story of any other human. You may be amazed at what you find out.

May I add, this translation does not seek to question the validity of any traditional translation. It simply offers a basic historical foundation, as Luke says, 'to get the issue straight.'

PART ONE: THE BIG STORY

1 Luke's introduction

[Luke 1.1-4]

The Jews have done it! They've cracked the problem of evil. They've shown what true humanity is, and become a light for the nations. Now, every human family can live a life of heaven-on-earth. This book tells how they did it.

The good Creator planned a heaven-on-earth for humans – so *The Law* and *The Prophets* say. But evil tricked people into worshipping stuff, and killed our true humanity. People made little gods of what they liked – war, booze, sex, power – and created murder and mayhem.

To save the planet, the good Creator took on Abraham. His job was to get society – and through it the environment – on course again. He signed the contract for his family, the twelve tribes of Jews, to do the work. And he was promised a land in which to do it.

When the family were made slaves in Egypt, the Creator-God rescued them. On Liberation day he freed them. The prophet Moses ordered the sea to part, and led them to safety in the desert. There he fed them with bread from heaven. He called them the 'son-of-God', and gave them *The Law* to help them keep their contract.

Moses' successor, Joshua (called Jesus in English) brought them through the river Jordan into the promised land. He drove out its idolatrous rulers, and established the family there. (The hero of this book was named after him – in hope that he would redo what Joshua had done!)

When the Jews broke their contract and were enslaved again, David defeated their enemy in single combat. He freed them, and ruled the nations all around. He took the national title 'son-of-God'. God promised that a son-of-David would rule over all nations.

They failed to save the planet

But again the Jews broke their contract and ten of the twelve tribes were lost. Idolatrous nations destroyed God's Temple, and made them slaves – in exile from God. But prophets promised that God would return to them and make a new contract. He would give them a new heart and spirit, to do the job. The dead-and-done-for nation would, they said, be resurrected.

When an idolatrous overlord set up an image in the Temple, it sparked a revolt. Led by a family nick-named the Hammerers, they cleansed the Temple. Their martyrs died under terrible torture. They claimed that after victory, they'd be resurrected in the age to come.

But victory didn't bring the age to come. It just replaced corrupt foreign rulers with corrupt Hammerers. The people splintered into quarrel-

ling sects, and ended up under the iron heel of the
Roman Emperor.

But the dream lived on

Yet they still dreamed of the day when God
would forgive their ancestors' sins. A forerunner
would precede God's return. A son-of-David
would liberate the poor people, and judgement
day would arrive for the idolaters. Feasting would
replace fasting. The blind would see, the deaf
hear, and the sick be healed.

The son-of-David would rule in Jerusalem,
and deal with the evil they suffered. He would
set up his government for ever, and rebuild God's
Temple. But before victory over the enemy, there
would be terrible suffering. No easy way could
bring peace, justice, and a renewed environment.

People looked for signs of a son-of-David, and
many would-be-rulers offered signs. They mim-
icked Moses by going into the desert, or Joshua
crossing the Jordan. They gathered followers, and
marched on Jerusalem. But all lacked the one sign
they needed – to start like David by defeating
their enemy.

Some patriots lived as freedom-fighters in
remote caves. Others joined sects waiting for the
moment to strike, when the signs were right. Others went along with their overlords and puppet
rulers – and did well for themselves.

But most thought only of surviving in a hard, cruel world, and joined no party. They had their community at the local meeting place, and the yearly festivals in Jerusalem. They might long for liberation, but – with the Roman puppet-ruler Herod – they had no choice. They just put up with things, and got on with their lives.

It was into this disparate Jewish society that Jesus of Nazareth was born. With many versions of his life now current, it seems time for a serious historical account. I, Luke, have therefore researched all the evidence from eyewitnesses and record takers. This offers a secure basis for you to get the whole issue straight.

PART TWO: THE UPRISING BEGINS

2 Evil Empire, your time is up!

[1.5-2.52]

Herod the first was a clever thug, good at killing High Priests, babies, terrorists, his in-laws, sons or wives. To tame the Jews, the Emperor made him their ruler – but noted, 'I'd rather be Herod's pig than his son.' At least Herod was Jewish enough not to butcher pigs.

For forty years the half-Jew terrorised his people, and they hated him. To prove his right to be their ruler, he set out to rebuild the Temple. For God had commanded a ruler to build the Temple, and only the ruler could rebuild it.

But the taxes needed to build this eighth wonder of the world, made him hated even more. To stop everyone cheering at his death, he arranged for the best-loved people to be assassinated. His last act was to kill yet one more of his sons.

It was in Herod's dying days, that a virgin peasant girl, named Mary, became pregnant. Her village of Nazareth was a nationalist hotbed in the northern hill country. There, every peasant girl dreamt that her baby would lead the liberation struggle. And Mary had cause, for she was engaged to Joseph, a descendant of King David.

A strange messenger, Mary said, had foretold her pregnancy. He had built her dreams by saying that her baby would be the promised ruler. As son-of-David, he would take the title, son-of-God. With countless other hopeful peasant girls, she would name her baby Jesus. He would be a new Joshua – defeat their enemies, and lead them into the promised land. Even in her womb, Mary fed her baby the national dream:

'The Almighty has acted through me!' she sang out. 'He's remembered his promise to help us. Our tyrants are about to be overthrown! We, the poor oppressed, are going to be the rulers now!'

Others of her family bore the names of the revolutionary Hammerer leaders. Her cousin Elizabeth named her baby 'Our-God-is-coming-back' (called John in English). His father cried out:

'Praise be to our God, he's about to liberate us! My son is the promised forerunner of God's ruler. God has forgiven us! He's back with us!'

This baby was to become John-the-Immerser. But his birth copied an ancient prophet's who foretold the destruction of the first Temple – a bad omen for the present corrupt rulers and Temple. Yet this was also a good omen, for that same prophet had also secretly anointed David ruler.

A son-of-David must be born in David's town, Bethlehem. So the Emperor, though unaware, prepared for his own replacement. He declared a census. It forced Mary and Joseph to return to Bethlehem to register.

In contrast to Rome's imperial pomp, the lowest witnessed the new ruler's birth – a sign of their coming liberation. The baby's first outing was therefore to the Temple, to pledge him to his task. As Jesus was carried in, an elderly seer took the baby in his arms. He prophesied: 'this child will liberate the people, and light the way for the nations.' Yet he added a fateful warning. The child would be opposed by many of his own people. He would be a sign of both destruction and resurrection.

His parents returned to Nazareth, to bring up their child like any other boy in the village. He learned well the story of *The Law* and *The Prophets* – and his people's role. He was quick to accept the family commitment to God's government. As he approached his teens, the issue erupted violently.

The Emperor appointed a new regional Governor, and a new census was ordered, to raise taxes. The announcement inflamed a Jewish revolutionary. Jews were ruled by God, he said, and paid taxes only to God – not to the Emperor.

With a gang of desperadoes, he seized the armoury in the capital of the North. The city was barely five miles from Nazareth, and there he proclaimed 'God as ruler'. It took two years for the Roman armies to arrive. They reduced the city to the ground. Guilty and innocent alike suffered crucifixion.

The victims' agony of nails through the hands and feet was nothing. The real torture was of the lungs. Every breath increased it. And the ignominy itself was worse than death. But worst of all, *The Law* put the curse of God on such people. Crosses across the land put paid to serious revolt by Jews for sixty years.

The revolt set off a strong debate. When his parents took the twelve-year-old Jesus to the Liberation Festival in Jerusalem, they lost him there. They found him in the Temple, tackling the authorities about God's government. All the teachers were fazed by the boy's questions and ideas.

When scolded by his parents he was unrepentant. 'Didn't you expect me to get on with the job?' he replied.

Back home in Nazareth the youngster was an obedient son, respected by everyone. He grew taller and wiser with the years, and chafed at the injustice his people suffered. Many sects offered him their way to right their wrongs. Each used the bits in the books of *The Law* and *The Prophets* that suited them.

But the youth was getting his own ideas of how to complete their story. Everyone wanted rid of the Romans, but Jesus saw that God cared equally for all. He provided sun and rain for the just – and the unjust. Their Father God cared equally for Romans!

He watched as would-be-rulers set themselves up, gathered followers, and marched on Jerusalem. He too thought Roman rule should end. But he was discerning a different way to win. His mother had brought him up to defeat their oppressor. Her dream was not enough – he needed to have the conviction in himself. By the time that certainty came, he was over thirty.

3 The Empire is defeated, God's rule arrives

[3.1 – 5.16]

Herod hadn't managed to kill all his sons before he died. The Emperor had made one of them ruler of the North, and the Jordan valley. The Prince renamed himself Herod II, and wasn't having any talk of other rulers. Such talk spelt death.

The Emperor – self-styled 'son-of-god', 'saviour', and 'bringer of peace' – ruled the South through a Governor. He had appointed Pilate, a tactless and brutal man. Pilate's crass decrees increased people's bitterness against Rome. Only the threat of national revolt stopped him seizing the Temple treasury.

Violent revolutionaries had to stay underground for now, but loyal Jews were still expecting freedom. The age-to-come, their teachers assured them, would soon arrive. It was an auspicious time for Jesus of Nazareth to enter onto the world stage.

The uprising began when his cousin John came in from the desert with great news. God, he announced, was forgiving their sins of serving other gods, and was returning to them. All through the Jordan valley John proclaimed that the end of exile under idolaters was at hand.

Those who responded were immersed by John in the Jordan to mark them as the real Jews. They'd enter the promised land under God's rule in the new age. In this way he fulfilled what the prophet foretold of the ruler's forerunner:

> The voice of someone shouting in the desert:
>
> 'Get ready a road fit for our God!
>
> Get the crooked straight, and the rough levelled.
>
> Every living thing shall see God's highway to victory!'

People came out in droves to be immersed by John.

'You brood of snakes,' he bawled at them, 'who warned you to flee from the coming destruction? Prove that you're different by the way you live! Don't think, "Because we're Jews, we'll be given God's government." God can make Jews out of these stones! This generation is a tree that produces no fruit. It will be felled as fuel for the fire. The axe is ready to cut it down to the roots.'

'Then what shall we do?' the crowds asked.

'If you have two coats,' he said, 'share with someone without one. Do the same thing with your food.'

'What shall we do?' tax collectors asked.

'Be honest. Collect no more than is due,' he replied.

'What shall we do?' soldiers asked him.

'Don't blackmail people for money,' he told them. 'You get paid well enough, be content with your pay.'

Expectations grew, and people began to wonder whether John might be the promised ruler. But John settled the matter:

'I only immerse you in water,' he said. 'Someone stronger is coming. He'll plunge you into the coming age, where God's spirit transforms you – or else he'll cremate you! He'll gather the fruit, but the rubbish he'll burn on the tip.'

The crowds knew who 'the rubbish' were – the High Priestly clans and wealthy landowning lords. His words sealed their fate, for to his hearers, John was a prophet.

But when John rejected Herod as ruler for stealing his brother's wife, Herod struck. He locked John in his dungeon. 'Herod's brother's wife', as John called her, made sure he never came out again. The lady, named Herodias, was not one to be crossed. She had married Herod's brother, expecting him to be made ruler. So when Herod came to stay, she seduced him. She made Herod agree to get rid of his wife. But Herod's wife got wind of things. She escaped back to her outraged father, the ruler of Arabia. In the war that followed, Herod suffered a disastrous defeat.

'This disaster was God's punishment,' all the people said, 'for the evil Herod did to John.' The Emperor then added his own punishment, and sentenced Herod to the misery of exile. All Herodias' feminine charms failed to save him. The conniving pair lost everything – but this has jumped us ahead of our story.

Jesus had been among those John immersed, and at that moment John had unknowingly anointed him ruler. For as Jesus prayed in the river, he knew God's Spirit was with him – as his ancestor David had known at his anointing. The words God had given David rang in Jesus' ears:

You're my chosen ruler.

Today, I've become your Father.

That settled any doubts, and summoned him to action. He *was* now the ruler who must reign in Jerusalem. *He* must set up God's rule on earth once and for all. *He* had to carry out God's plan in *The Law* and *The Prophets* – and work out the way to do it. His ancestor David was titled son-of-God. But all humans were created to be sons-of-God. Our true humanity was lost by our inhumanity – serving man-made gods. The promised ruler needed to restore our true humanity, by showing himself to be a son-of-God.

As the ruler, Jesus *was* the nation – what he did, the Jews did. He alone could:

- demonstrate God's forgiveness of his people's sins, by defeating the evil ruler who oppressed them,

- bring back the lost tribes, resurrect his people, heal the sick, turn their fasts into feasts,

- rule in Jerusalem, renew their contract with God, rebuild God's Temple, set up God's rule on earth – and bring in the age to come with a new creation.

Since the day Moses led the liberated people into the desert, the desert itself shrieked, 'Liberation!' Like John, Jesus was impelled to launch his revolution there. Luckily for him, the Romans hadn't yet caught on that 'Jews + desert = trouble'.

To signal his intent, Jesus copied Moses at the first liberation: he fasted forty days. But his next stroke was unheard-of, and upturned everyone's idea of their enemy. Their enemy was the evil Roman Emperor – the cause of all the evils they suffered. And David had taught them how to deal with evil people: 'Go after the evildoers until the last one of them is destroyed.'

But Jesus had seen that using evil means to defeat evil, simply doubled the evil. All the false would-be-rulers went down that seductive path. Jesus saw the enemy was not evil people, but evil itself. Evil had led astray the Romans – and equally his people! – he must defeat evil itself. And the fight must begin in himself.

Evil struck first. It offered him a triple-win ticket – to end his hunger, remove all doubts about his role, and make him as great as Moses.

'If you're really the ruler,' evil queried, 'and the title son-of-God is really yours, act like Moses did in the desert. Order this stone to turn into bread.'

Jesus decided that the only way to win was to follow God's plan.

'It's more than bread that's needed,' he threw back. '*The Law* states: "obeying God's every word brings God's government."'

That trumped evil's first attempt. So it tried again, flashing a picture of the mighty Emperors of the earth through Jesus' mind. He could be the greatest, and have all a man could dream of.

'All this power,' evil promised him, 'all this celebrity can be yours if you'll just be practical. Every ruler has to serve his own self-interest.'

'*The Law* states,' Jesus responded, 'You shall serve the Lord, your God, and him alone.'

That got rid of that one, but evil had a final ploy. It had defeated the Jews when, newly-declared son-of-God, Moses had led them into the desert. There they had put God to the test. So evil tried the same trick with this newly-declared son-of-God.

'When you reach Jerusalem,' evil queried, 'you could throw yourself off the top of the Temple. Doesn't the prophet say, "He will order his angels to look after you – they'll see you don't hurt your foot on anything"? That'll prove you're the ruler!'

'*The Law* says,' Jesus hit back, killing the thought, '"You shall not try to make God do what you want."'

It was a decisive blow. Evil fled the field – to wait for a better chance. The victory proved that the ancestors' sins of serving other gods were forgiven. God was back with his servant! Jesus returned to his house in Capernaum a free man, governed by God. God's rule over his people had begun.

But great news for the people was bad news for Herod. If news of a new ruler spread, Jesus would join John in Herod's dungeon. Yet if Jesus was to reign in Jerusalem, he had to gather followers. So the Jewish family needed to hear the great news.

The news his neighbours in Capernaum wanted was of victory over the Romans. Yet they could see that Jesus had become a very different young man. He compelled attention, and when he started healing the sick, this turned to astonishment.

Word spread quickly, and he began teaching in meeting places all through the area. By the time he returned to Nazareth, people were seeing him as a prophet. And as he always did on the holy day, he went to the meeting place there. The book of the prophet Isaiah was passed to him, and he read the passage:

> The Spirit of God has appointed me to give the great news:
>
> - God's return to his poor people
> - the end of his people's exile
> - recovery of sight for the blind
> - freedom for the oppressed
> - the year when all are forgiven

He closed the book, gave it back to the attendant, and prepared to speak. Everyone in the meeting place was agog to hear when this longed for moment would arrive.

'Today,' he announced, 'these words have been fulfilled. God has forgiven sins. Our exile is over.'

This was what they wanted to hear.

'He has unbreakable love,' Jesus continued, quoting the words of David, 'and his gracious forgiveness is for all. All people shall share his government.'

Forgiveness for *all people*? This was *not* what they wanted to hear. God's gracious forgiveness was for them, and certainly not for Romans! For their oppressors there would be no forgiveness, only judgement. The whole place reacted in shock.

'What's he saying?' they murmured. 'He doesn't sound like a son of Joseph. None of his family would say such things. He's not one of us. How can he be a prophet?'

'No doubt,' Jesus responded, 'you're going to quote me the old saying, "Start at home, Doctor. We've heard what you did in Capernaum, so do the same here." Well I'll tell you another old saying: "No prophet is ever accepted in his own country."'

They were nonplussed.

'Remember,' Jesus pressed on, 'in the days of the prophet Elijah there was a famine. There were many Jewish widows then, but the prophet Elijah was sent to none of them. He was sent to a foreign widow in another country.'

That really offended them.

'And there were many Jewish lepers in the time of Elisha,' he added, ignoring rising tension. 'None of them were healed. The only leper healed was a foreign general, commanding an invading army.'

Goaded to fury at the thought of God prefer-ring an idolatrous invader to them, they erupted.

They hustled him out of the village to throw him over the edge of the hill. But he went through the middle of them, and got safely away.

Evil had lost the battle in the desert, but this time it had nearly finished him. If Jesus was to go on living, he had to learn quickly. As well as being harmless as a dove, he would need to be wise as a serpent.

The next holy day he was teaching in the meeting place at Capernaum. Their struggle, he was telling them, was against evil itself, and he had defeated evil in the desert. They were astounded, because he spoke as if he had authority.

But a man in the meeting – who the whole town thought possessed by a 'demon' – suddenly uttered an unearthly howl.

'A-a-a-a-h! Back off, Jesus of Nazareth!' the man yelled at the top of his voice. 'Have you come here to destroy us? I know who you are. You're God's anointed ruler of the Jews!'

'Shut up and get out of him!' Jesus commanded the man's 'demon'.

At that, the man collapsed to the floor in the middle of everyone. Then it seemed that the 'demon' had come out of him, without doing the man any harm. Everyone was stunned.

'What's happening?' they began whispering. 'He seems to have power and authority to drive out demons!'

And the news spread like wildfire. After he left the meeting, he went to his neighbour Simon's home. He arrived to find Simon's mother-in-law in a high fever. When they asked Jesus to do something for her, he ordered the fever out. It left her at once, and she got up and began to look after them.

After sunset when the holy day ended, people brought all their sick to him. No matter what the disease, he laid his hands on each one and healed them. 'Demons' came out of many of them.

'You're the ruler of the Jews!' the 'demons' screeched, 'the son-of-God!'

Jesus shut them up at once. He had never said he was the ruler, and their shrieks endangered him. At daybreak the next day, he left Capernaum for a deserted place. But when people realised he'd gone, they went looking for him, and tried to stop him leaving.

'I have to go,' he told them. 'I have to announce the great news to all our towns.'

Then he left to spread the news to the South. But to Governor Pilate in the South, 'God's government' meant 'no taxes'. It was the talk of 'holy revolutionaries', and he had crosses ready to deal with them.

Jesus' subversion of the violent revolutionaries' idea set him to collide with them. He was on a knife edge between rulers and revolutionaries. He needed protection from both sides. So he copied his ancestor David, and enlisted three bodyguards.

It was one day after his return north. As he addressed the crowds by the lake, people were pressing in on every side. Fishermen were washing their nets on the shore, so Jesus got into Simon's boat. He asked him to push out a little, and sat addressing the crowds from the boat.

When he finished, he turned and said to Simon, 'Put out into deep water, and let your nets down for a catch.'

'Sir,' Simon replied, 'we've caught nothing all night. But if you say so, I'll let the nets down again.' They did, and the huge catch began to break the nets. They had to signal to their partners to come out and help them. Even then both boats were so full that they almost sank.

Simon fell down at Jesus' knees. 'Leave me alone, Sir,' he said, 'I'm no use to you.' Both crews were awe-struck at the size of the catch. So too were Simon's partners, James and John.

'Don't be scared,' Jesus told him. 'From now on your job will be to haul in drowning people! Our people are sunk, and you'll have to resurrect them as real Jews.'

After they'd brought their boats on shore, these three men gave up everything to become his bodyguards. They believed that they'd found the man to get rid of their oppressor, and resurrect their nation. And others soon joined them as his trainees.

To the violent revolutionaries, he was resurrecting the wrong people – like the disabled and diseased. These people, the revolutionaries thought, were lost to the real Jewish family. But to Jesus they were 'the lost tribes returning', as prophets foretold.

One day a leper saw him, and fell face down before him.

'Master,' the untouchable begged, 'you have the power to make me clean again, if only you want to.'

'I do want to. Be clean,' Jesus replied, touching the man.

Everyone watched in shock, then gasped. For instead of making Jesus 'unclean', the man was cleansed, his leprosy gone.

'Don't tell anyone,' Jesus ordered him, 'before you've done what *The Law* states. Go and show yourself to the priest, and make the required offering. It will prove to them that the liberation, which *The Law* of Moses promised, is now here.'

So, more than ever, word about him spread everywhere. The size of the crowds coming to hear him and be healed grew and grew. To get time in quiet, he had to escape to any isolated place alone. But along with all the acclaim, sinister forces began to appear.

PART THREE: PREPARING THE PEOPLE FOR VICTORY

4 The counter-attacks begin

[5.17 – 7.50]

Jesus had become a threat to the 'holy revolutionaries'. The reaction against him in Nazareth had been spontaneous, but now he faced organised opposition. It was led by the most popular sect of the Violent Revolutionary Idolatrous Nationalists (VRIN). The VRIN read just the bits of their bible that they liked:

> The fourth beast will be put to death. The truly human will rule over all races and nations forever.

The 'fourth beast', they claimed, was the Roman Empire. They were 'the truly human'. So they'd destroy the Roman Empire; then 'rule over all races and nations for ever'.

One day the VRIN arrived in force to tackle him. They came from north and south, with their legal experts from Jerusalem. The same day four men arrived carrying a paralysed man on his mattress. They wanted to lay him in front of Jesus, but they couldn't get through the crowd. So they took the man up on the roof, and removed some tiles. Then they let him down through the gap, mattress and all, right in front of Jesus.

'You're one of God's people,' Jesus said to him. 'God has forgiven his people's sins, so your sins are forgiven.'

The VRIN were aghast: if God had forgiven their sins, they would have defeated the Romans. The man must be claiming to forgive sins himself. It was blasphemy!

Jesus saw what they were thinking, and looked straight at them.

'The prophet says,' he reminded them, 'healing and forgiveness happen when God resurrects his people. You think this man's as good as dead, so what do you want me to say? "Your sins are forgiven," or "Join the resurrection of God's people, get up and walk"? But to prove that God's rule is arriving, and his servant has authority to proclaim it...'

[he paused and turned to the paralysed man,]

'I tell you,' Jesus said to him, 'God's people are being resurrected. Rise up, and take your mattress off home.'

Immediately, the paralysed man joined the resurrected Jews. He got up in front of them all! Then he picked up his mattress and went home, acclaiming what God had done. Everyone was thunderstruck.

'We've seen something incredible today,' people said.

And there was no way the VRIN could deny it. It was a brilliant advertisement that God was back with them. People went back to their villages carrying the news everywhere.

And to rub in that God had forgiven his people's sins, Jesus went to the customs post.

Everyone regarded tax collectors as sinners. To the VRIN they were also traitors. Jesus found the tax collector, named Levi, sitting at his post.

'Join me,' he said to him.

Levi at once rose to the challenge, and joined Jesus' resurrected people. To celebrate God's rule arriving, he arranged a huge feast. His house was packed with tax collectors and other sinners. It was a mighty demonstration that God had forgiven the people's sins.

The VRIN and their legal experts were out-raged. But it gave them an easy target. They began picking off Jesus' trainees.

'What are you doing,' they muttered to them, 'celebrating with sick traitors? We're the real Jews. We'll get God's government.'

Jesus saw what the VRIN were up to.

'If you're healthy,' Jesus rejoined, 'you won't need a doctor, only the sick do. I'm not here to call those on the right track to do a rethink, just those who've got it wrong.'

If Jesus was right, the VRIN were wrong – they were 'the sick' – and the sick were not real Jews at all! Their response was sharp.

'Haven't you noticed,' they sneered, 'that we're still under Roman rule? John's trainees know it. Look what's happened to him. They fast to pray for liberation, and so do our trainees. But look at yours, they're celebrating as if we've been liber-ated!'

'Because,' Jesus answered, 'fasts turn to feasts when God's rule arrives. You can't stop God's people celebrating God's return. It's the marriage feast of God and his people. Do you want people to fast at the wedding breakfast with the bridegroom present?'

'If God is present,' they scoffed, 'why are we still ruled by Rome? This is the time for fasting.'

'Your time for fasting,' Jesus warned them, 'will come. Don't think God will save you when your war with Rome starts.'

'The new age,' he told the crowd, 'is already here, like a new coat. But the VRIN want to cut it up to patch their old worn out way. The old and new don't match.' But the VRIN kept on repeating the old way.

'They're drunk on the old,' Jesus told his trainees. 'Like old drunks they keep mumbling, "Old wine is best." They want to put the new wine in the old skins of war for the land. But new wine bursts old skins, and you lose both. And they're going to lose both God's rule and the land.'

These skirmishes doubled the VRIN's concern. On the holy day they spied on Jesus as he went through some wheat fields. They saw his trainees pluck some ears of grain. The trainees rubbed the husk off to eat them. No work was allowed on the holy day, so they jumped out to confront him.

'Why,' they demanded, 'are your trainees working? They're grinding corn on the holy day!'

'Haven't you read the story of David,' Jesus chided them. 'His men ate the Temple bread, which only priests are allowed to eat. David himself gave it to them. But idolatrous spies reported this to the false ruler, and brought that Temple's destruction. Are you trying to do the same?'

'Does he think he's the son of David?' the VRIN smirked. 'When is he going to liberate us? When will we see our idolatrous enemy face the day of judgement?'

'God's servant is already bringing liberation,' Jesus replied, 'the day of judgement for the idolatrous is here.'

This added to the VRIN's anger, and the next Sabbath they waited for him in the synagogue. A man with a withered right hand was sat in the middle. They watched to see if Jesus would heal him. Jesus saw at once what was going on.

'Join the resurrected Jews,' Jesus said to the man, 'stand up here.' He got up, and stood there. Jesus looked round at everyone.

'Is the holy day given to do good or evil?' he asked. 'Is it, as *The Law* says, given to signal our liberation – or our destruction and exile?'

The VRIN were stuck. The Sabbath, *The Law* said, was a sign of liberation. Therefore to free people was to do good – to prevent it was to do evil. There was a tense silence.

'Stretch out your hand,' Jesus said to the man. As the man did so, his hand was restored.

The VRIN were wild. They went off to work out how to deal with this man. But his next move was a masterstroke that upstaged them all. For the Jewish family never forgot they were once twelve tribes. They still clung to the promise, that the lost tribes would be restored. So Jesus created a walking advertisement, that the lost tribes were now found!

The idea came to him one night, praying on a mountain. At dawn he called his trainees up to join him. Then he chose twelve of them from opposing groups – a visual broadcast that he was resurrecting the Jewish family. He named them his 'envoys'.

When he came down the mountain, he stopped at a level place. He was surrounded by a large number of followers. There was a huge crowd from all over, including Jerusalem – some even from abroad. Everyone wanted to hear what he was saying.

Many had come to be healed of diseases, and he healed them all. Those troubled with unclean spirits were cured, and the whole crowd wanted to touch him. Then he began to speak. He looked straight at his trainees, and announced:

First, who would share God's sovereignty, and who wouldn't:

> You're the poor downtrodden people, promised God's government. Your hunger for God's rule will be satisfied. You weep at the idolatry making Jerusalem a hell. You – not the powerful wealthy – will have the last laugh.

Lucky you when people hate you, cold-shoulder, slander, and warn others against you because of me. That's how their ancestors treated *The Prophets*. It's a sign that God is with you – celebrate and jump for joy!

But heaven help the rich landowners. When war with Rome starts, they've had it. Heaven help those who've got everything: they're going to lose the lot. And heaven help those who laugh at warnings of destruction. You're going to shed bitter tears.

And God help you if everybody likes you. Your ancestors loved the false prophets.

Second, his policy – how to share God's rule under the Romans:

To those who'll listen I say: love the Romans. If they hate you, curse and abuse you, give them back only good. Give them the very best, and pray for your abusers.

If they treat you like dirt, show true human dignity. If a soldier takes your coat, let him have your shirt as well. If they demand something, let them have it. If they take something, don't demand it back. Drown them in your generosity! Do to them what you would want them to do to you.

If you love those who love you, what use is that? Even Romans love those who love them. If you only help those who help you, what use is that? Even Romans do that. And if you lend hoping to get something out of it, what use is that? They'll lend to get something out of it.

Love the Romans, help them, lend to them, and don't expect to get anything back. Then you'll have the true humanity you claim to have, and be governed by God. Because God is loving towards ungrateful, grasping people. So be compassionate to the Romans, because your Father cares passionately about them.

Don't itch for the day when God sits in judgement on the Romans. If you do, his judgement will fall on you! You will be destroyed, not the Romans. But if you forgive the Romans, God will forgive you and govern you.

If you give only good to them, God will give you his everlasting government in full measure. He will pour it out for you neat, beyond anything you can imagine. It's your choice.

Finally, he gave warnings against following the VRIN:

The VRIN are leading people towards war with Rome, and they'll fall into that pit together. People don't know any better, because it's all they're taught.

You VRIN see a splinter in another Jew's eye. But you don't see the tree trunk in your own! You condemn others, but can't see how wrong you are yourselves. You're hypocrites. First, take that trunk out of your own eye and change your foreign policy. Then you'll see how to help your brothers put right their mistakes.

The true servant of God doesn't foment chaos. You don't get honest government by corrupt means – grapes don't come from thorns or figs from brambles. The fruit people produce will show who the real servant of God is.

If you really want God to govern, you act with true humanity. You create what's good for everyone. But those hooked by evil bring tragedy – and you can tell which is which by the way people talk.

Why do you call me, 'Master, Master,' when you don't do what I tell you? You go on hating the Romans. My follower hears what I'm saying and does it. Like a man building on rock. When the Roman flood rises, and the Roman armies come, his foundations won't shift.

But those who don't act on what I say are like those who hope the Temple will save them. They're

> building on ground with no foundation. When the
> Roman flood breaks against that Temple it'll utterly
> collapse. All that's left will be a vast ruin.

After these prophetic words Jesus went back
to Capernaum, where a Roman officer had heard
about him. The officer asked the local Jewish leaders to make a humble request - would Jesus please
come, for his slave was near death. The officer
had high regard for his slave, and the community
leaders pleaded his case strongly:

'You ought to do this for him,' they told Jesus,
'because he loves our people. He even built us our
meeting house.'

Jesus went with them, but when he got near
the house the officer sent a message: 'Sir, please
don't trouble to come any further. I'm not a Jew,
so I didn't presume to come to you myself. Just
give the order and let my slave be healed. Like
yourself, I'm used to authority, and I have soldiers
under me. I say to one, "Go," and he goes; and to
my slave, "Do this," and he does it.'

When Jesus heard this he was astonished at
the man's trust in him. He turned to the crowd
following him.

'I tell you,' he said, 'I haven't found any Jew
who trusts me as much as this man.'

He gave the order, and by the time the messengers got back, the slave was well again. It was a
sign that the nations would share in the new age.

But Jesus' task was to resurrect his fellow Jews,
and he came to a town called Nain. He was followed by a big crowd. As he arrived, the corpse of

a widow's only son was being carried out. A large crowd of mourners were with her. When Jesus saw her he was deeply moved.

'Stop mourning,' he said to her.

Then he astounded everyone: he went up to the bier and touched it. Touching the dead defiled a man, and the bearers stopped in their tracks. Then Jesus spoke to the corpse.

'Young man,' he said, 'I tell you, rise up.'

The dead man sat up, and began talking! Jesus helped him off the bier, and gave him back to his mother. The crowd's reaction was electric: 'He's done what the prophet Elijah did,' they said. 'Elijah has come to herald God's return, as *The Prophets* promised.'

News of what Jesus had done spread through the whole of the South. John's trainees gave John the news, but it wasn't the news John was waiting for. He was expecting Jesus to liberate the nation, and free all prisoners like himself. So John sent two of his followers to question Jesus.

When they arrived they found Jesus healing all kinds of people, and giving sight to the blind.

'John has sent us,' they said, 'to ask, "Are you the one who's going to liberate the country, or have we got to wait for someone else?"'

To answer yes or no would have confirmed John's wrong ideas.

'Go and tell John,' Jesus told them, 'what you've seen and heard – the blind see, the deaf hear, and the lame walk. Lepers are cleansed, the dead are raised up, and the poor are given the great news.'

This was what *The Prophets* had promised, but John was looking for something else. So Jesus added:

'Those sharing God's government don't find fault with me.'

It was a strong challenge to John. His days in Herod's dungeon were numbered. He was soon to be beheaded. After John's messengers had left, Jesus began speaking to the crowds about him.

'When you went out into the desert,' he asked them, 'what were you looking for? A reed shaken by the wind?'

That was just a laugh. Everyone knew the reed was code for Herod. He bent like a reed with every wind that blew. Were they really looking for a ruler like Herod? 'Heaven forbid!' was the response.

'Then what were you looking for?' Jesus asked again. 'A man bedecked in purple, living in luxury? If you want a ruler like that, you can find one in any palace.'

They'd had enough of those. 'So what did you go out looking for?' Jesus asked again, 'A prophet?'

'Yes,' was the answer.

'And you were right!' Jesus said. 'But John was more than a prophet. He is the forerunner,

promised by *The Prophets*. He fulfils the prophecy
that says:

> I will send the prophet Elijah ahead of you, to get
> things ready.

'No one has ever had a greater role than John
– yet someone with the smallest grasp of God's
government now has a greater role.'

When the crowd heard this, everyone – even
the tax collectors – agreed with him about John.
They'd accepted John's message. It was the VRIN
and the rulers who'd rejected John – they'd
rejected John for fasting, and were now rejecting
Jesus for feasting!

'They're like grumpy children,' Jesus said,
'nothing suits them. John didn't drink wine or
eat bread, so the VRIN said, "There's a demon
in him!" Now, because I celebrate God's return
with feasts, they say, "This son's a glutton and
drunkard. *The Law* says: put such a son to death!"
But God's way is proved right by all those who
obey him.'

The VRIN were unmoved, but the response of
the crowds was the same everywhere. People kept
flocking to him, and talking about him. So a VRIN
named Simon decided to see for himself if Jesus
was a prophet. He invited Jesus to dine with him.

Jesus was reclining at the meal, when a notori-
ous woman in the town came in. She had heard
he was there, and had brought an expensive jar
of ointment. As she stood at his feet sobbing,
her tears began to wet his feet. Then she undid
her hair – which no decent woman would do in

public – and wiped his feet with her hair. Then she kissed his feet, and anointed them with the ointment.

Simon watched all this thinking, 'If he was a prophet he'd have known that she's a sinner.' So Jesus, seeing what his host was thinking, said:

'Simon, I've got something to ask you.'

'Please do, teacher,' Simon replied.

'A moneylender had two debtors. One owed him a huge amount and the other not much. When neither could pay he forgave both debts. So which do you think will love him more?'

'I suppose the one he forgave the most,' Simon replied.

'You're right,' Jesus told him.

And turning towards the woman, he said to Simon:

'You see what this woman has done. When I arrived at your house, you offered me no water to wash my feet. But she has washed them with her tears, and dried them with her hair. You gave me no respectful welcome, but she has abased herself in welcoming me. She has recognised my authority, but you didn't.

'Her great love shows how much she's been forgiven. Those refusing God's forgiveness cannot love him, and don't obey the first commandment, 'Love God'. So they cannot share his government.'

Jesus turned to the woman.

'Your sins are forgiven,' he told her.

This was too much for the VRIN guests. 'Who does he think he is,' they muttered to each other, 'claiming to forgive sins?'

So Jesus rubbed it in.

'You trust,' Jesus told the woman, 'that God is using me to bring about his government. So you have a share in it. Go in peace.'

After that some VRIN were even ready to work with Herod's men to get rid of him. This increased the danger from Herod. But Jesus' strategy kept him ahead of them.

5 The rightful ruler plans to upturn everything

[8.1–9.50]

Jesus was copying his ancestor David, when David was on the run from the false ruler. Jesus too kept on the move, and stuck to small towns and villages. It was too risky to attract attention in the cities. And as if threats from Herod and the VRIN weren't enough, he faced other issues.

Jesus was upsetting the gender roles of society. He took many women he'd healed with him – like Mary Magdalen freed from 'seven demons', and Joanna (the wife of Herod's household manager!). They used their own money to provide for him.

The risk from Herod grew with the size of the crowds. To avoid joining John in Herod's dungeon, Jesus was giving the great news in coded stories. That way only those open to it would get the meaning.

He told the crowds: 'A sower went out sowing his seed. Some fell on the path and got trampled. Some the birds ate. Some withered on rocky soil, and some were choked by thorns. But some fell on good soil where it produced a vast harvest.' To mark that he was speaking in code he would add: 'Those who have ears that can hear, let them hear.'

When his trainees asked for the key to the code, Jesus told them: 'You are the harvest of people governed by God. Your privilege is to know the secret of God's sovereignty. But coded stories confuse those against it. That's why the prophet Isaiah says:

> though they look, they won't see it;
>
> and though they hear, they won't get it;
>
> because they're set on serving man-made gods.

Isaiah also tells us how long they'll go on like this:

> until their cities are ruins, and the land becomes a wilderness.

But Isaiah affirms:

> God's rule will grow from a seed under a charred stump that's left.

Then Jesus unlocked the code: it was the Jews' story. God, the sower, sowed word of his rule by prophet after prophet. But the harvest of heaven-on-earth never came. Those:

- on the path heard the words, but evil closed their minds, and they weren't freed

- on the rocky soil were keen while it was popular, but drew back when attacked

- in the thorns were choked by worry about property, money, or chasing pleasure

- on the good soil – honest, open-hearted people – now hear what's said and produce the harvest

The code, he assured them, would soon be open to all. The secret would be out. But with the harvest here, things were changing. Now the entry ticket was doing God's will – not being a Jew. The Jewish family's job was to be a light for the nations.

'No one hides a light under the bed,' he told the crowds, 'except the VRIN! They want to keep the light for themselves. A light is meant to show the way in to those who want to enter.'

But even his trainees still thought God's government was just for Jews. So Jesus pressed the issue.

'Make sure you hear what I'm saying,' he said. 'God will give more of his government to those who get it. But if anyone thinks he's got it because he's a Jew, he hasn't got it! He'll lose everything he's got, when the VRIN try to get it by war with the Romans.'

Back in Nazareth such talk was thought madness. The family's duty was to chain a madman in a dark inner room. Jesus' family came to take charge of him. But they couldn't get near because of the crowd, so sent a demand into the house.

'Your mother and your brothers are outside,' someone announced, 'they want to see you.'

But if – as society demanded – he went out to them, he knew what would happen. They would grab and bundle him back to Nazareth, never to be heard of again.

'My mother and my brothers?' Jesus asked, looking round. 'But they're here. My family hear what my Father says, and do it.'

It was a shocking and shattering answer. Being a racial Jew was no longer enough! Those doing God's will were now God's family. His family left for home without him. And Jesus began to train his men to give the great news to the idolatrous nations.

'We're going over the lake to idolatrous territory,' he told them soon afterwards.

And as they sailed across, Jesus fell asleep in the boat. While he was asleep a vicious wind struck the lake, and the trainees were terrified. They thought the evil forces of the sea were swamping the boat.

'Master! Master! we're sinking!' they cried.

Jesus woke up and ordered wind and waves to cease. Surging waves became calm.

'What are you thinking of?' he asked them. 'Don't you trust me to bring God's government on earth? Would God let me drown before the job's done?'

They were scared stiff and stupefied.

'Who is this man?' they whispered to each other. 'He acts like Moses, and gives orders to wind and waves – and they obey!'

It was a sign of the coming liberation Moses promised. With fresh faith in him, they sailed on.

As Jesus stepped onto foreign soil, a 'demon-possessed' man from the nearby town was there. The man's family had tried many times to lock him away. Each time he snapped his chains, and his 'demons' drove him into the desert. He now lived in the tombs, and hadn't worn clothes for a long time. He saw Jesus coming, screamed, and fell down in front of him.

'What do you want with me, King Jesus, Son of God?' the man yelled.

Jesus at once ordered the dirty spirit to get out.

'Please, please don't torment me,' howled the man.

'What's your name?' Jesus asked him.

'Army,' the man replied.

He was called Army because he had a whole army of 'demons' in him! And the 'demons' started pleading not to be sent into the depths of the earth. The man begged – in an unearthly voice – for them to enter a large herd of pigs, feeding there. At the sound, the pigs rushed in panic over the edge into the lake. The terrified herdsmen fled, and told everyone the pigs were drowned.

That brought all the town's people out, to see what was going on. They found the 'demon-possessed' man sitting at Jesus' feet as a trainee. And when they heard about the 'demons', they were frightened to death. They asked Jesus to go away, so he got into the boat to sail back across the lake.

The man freed from his 'demons' begged Jesus to let him come with him.

'Return home,' Jesus said, 'and tell them the story of what God has done for you.'

So the man went off telling everyone in the town, what Jesus had done for him. And Jesus sailed back across the lake with his trainees. They'd seen a new way to take on an idolatrous nation. Moses had drowned the Egyptians like dirty pigs – but Jesus had cleaned out the evil, and liberated the man. The trainees were to do the same for the nations.

Jesus returned to his task – to resurrect the Jews – and a crowd were there to welcome him. Jairus, leader of the local meeting place was in the crowd, and he fell at Jesus' feet. His twelve-year-old only daughter was dying. He implored Jesus to come to his house, and Jesus went with him.

A woman in the crowd behind had suffered internal bleeding for twelve years. She'd spent all she'd got on doctors and was no better. She reached through the crowd behind Jesus, and touched the hem of his cloak. As she did so she was healed.

Jesus swung round.

'Who touched me?' he asked.

Everyone looked blank.

'Sir,' Peter said, 'what do you mean, "who touched me"? You're almost being crushed by the crowd!'

'Someone touched me,' Jesus insisted. 'Power went out from me. I know it did.'

The woman saw she couldn't hide what she'd done, and was trembling. As an 'unclean' woman, she thought she'd made him 'unclean'. She fell down. In front of everyone she told him why she'd done it, and that she'd been healed!

'Daughter,' he said, 'your trust in me as God's promised liberator has set you free. Share the peace of God's sovereign rule.'

At the same moment, a man came running from the leader's house.

'Your daughter is dead,' the man told Jairus, 'don't trouble the teacher any more.'

'Have no fear!' Jesus said to Jairus, hearing the message. 'Trust me, and your daughter will win through.'

When he got to the house, everyone was out-side mourning.

'Stop this weeping!' Jesus told them, 'she's not dead, she's only asleep.'

But they laughed at him, because they knew she'd died. So Jesus stopped anyone going in with him, except the child's parents, Peter, John and James. Once inside he took hold of the girl's hand, and said very firmly.

'Get up, child.'

The girl's spirit returned, and she got up at once. Her parents couldn't believe their eyes. 'Give her something to eat,' he told them.

Then they knew she really was alive, and were completely overcome. But Jesus ordered them to tell no one what had happened.

His trainees were now nearly ready for him to make his final move. But before he could rule in Jerusalem, the nation must be alerted. So he took the twelve aside, to plan a lightning strike through the land. He gave them power to drive out evil spirits and cure diseases. They were to proclaim God as ruler, and move fast.

'Don't take anything for your journey,' he told them, 'not a thing. Stay at the first house that offers you a bed, and at dawn move on. If a village is bent on war, leave it. Shake off the dust of that idolatrous place as a warning to them. If they want to destroy the idolaters, the idolaters they'll destroy are themselves!'

So the twelve set off through all the villages, proclaiming that God's rule was arriving. They showed signs of it by healing people, and reports poured in to Herod. But he didn't know what to make of them. Some said John-the-Immerser had been raised from the dead. Others said the forerunner Elijah had appeared, or that one of the old prophets had risen.

'I cut John's head off,' Herod muttered. 'Who can this be I keep hearing about?' and he was keen to interrogate Jesus.

When his envoys reported all they'd done, Jesus took them on their own to a safe place. As they passed Bethsaida, he was spotted and word went round. Crowds came out into the desert after him, yet he welcomed them. He spoke to them about God's rule, and healed those with diseases.

When it was getting late, the twelve became impatient and got together.

'Send the crowd off,' they told him. 'They'll have to get food and lodging from the nearest villages and countryside. There's nothing for them here in this wilderness.'

'You give them something to eat,' Jesus replied.

'All we've got is five loaves and two fish,' they said. 'You don't want us to go and buy food for all these do you?' (There were about five thousand men there.)

'Get them to sit down in groups of fifty,' he told them.

Then he took the loaves and fish, looked to heaven and thanked God for the food. He divided it up, and began giving it to his trainees to pass round. Just as Moses had fed the people in the desert, so now everyone had enough. They even took up twelve wicker baskets full of bread left over.

But five thousand men in the desert – each with a weapon – could easily be swept away. He would find himself carried off by a mob, set on making him their ruler. His trainees would love it, so at once he packed them off across the lake. Then he slipped away into the hills by himself.

His idea of 'rulers' and 'God' upturned their idea of rulers and God. They all thought of God as a super-emperor. If he was on your side, the Romans stood no chance. But Jesus had seen that God coerced no one. His almighty power – the only power to right all wrongs – was different. He was not a cosmic enforcer, but had selfless pure love.

Every ruler sacrificed his people to save himself. But the almighty Creator-God, the Jews' Father, ruled as servant! As the son-of-God, Jesus must mirror his 'Father' and act as servant. He must be ready to give his own life, to save his people.

This was a cosmic shift in human thinking. It would make no sense to his trainees. But he must tell them, in hope that after his triumph they would recall what he'd said. Then they would grasp it, and call the nations to share God's government.

So after time in prayer, and with only his trainees around, he put the issue to them.

'Who are the crowds saying that I am?' he began.

'John-the-Immerser,' they replied. That was no surprise. Jesus' warnings sounded to people very like those of John.

'But some say,' they added, 'you're Elijah, the Forerunner. And others say you're one of the prophets of old risen from the dead.'

'What about you?' he asked them. 'Who are you going to tell people that I am?'

'God's promised ruler!' Peter blurted out.

Peter had let their cat out of the bag. They would talk of him as the ruler, and doom his mission. He would end up like the rest, leader of one more futile uprising. And there was no way to change their idea of a ruler. So he gave them the strictest order never to speak of him as a ruler.

'*The Prophets* decree,' he said, 'that to rule the world, God's servant must suffer. He'll be rejected by the ruling lords, chief priests and legal authorities. He'll be crucified, and on the third day rise again.'

None of them believed he meant it. *The Law* said crucifixion was a sign of God's curse on a man. It was the end, and they were sure Jesus was going to win. Yet he said the same to all those wanting to join him on his march to Jerusalem.

'If anyone wants to follow me,' he told them, 'he must reject all thought of self-interest. Every day he must be ready to face torture and death on a cross. Those out to get control of the land will end up dead. Those giving their lives for God's government with me will share it in the new age.

'What's the use of seizing the land, when you'll lose everything in a war with the Romans? When Rome wipes out the VRIN, it'll prove which of us is God's servant. People will see the glory of God's everlasting rule, and discover who the real servant is.

'I promise you,' he added, 'some of you here will see God's ruler installed.'

But was it the right plan? Had the moment come, he wondered. For if he had doubts about either, he would fail. And eight days later he went up a mountain to pray about it. He took Peter, John and James with him. As he prayed, his face looked different, and even his clothes looked sparkling white.

Peter and his fellow trainees seemed drugged with sleep. But they kept awake enough to see Jesus and two men standing together. The two men were there planning with him, Moses and Elijah. They looked glorious, and talked of the people's liberation, which Jesus was going to achieve in Jerusalem.

When he saw the two men were leaving, Peter said to Jesus, 'Master, it's wonderful for us to be here. Let's put up three shelters, one for you, one for Moses, and one for Elijah.'

He didn't know what he was saying, but as he said it a cloud came down. It covered them and they were terrified. Then they heard a voice out of the cloud. It echoed God's words to David, making him ruler over the nations:

> This is my Son, the one I've chosen. Listen to what he's telling you!

But even as the voice spoke there was only Jesus there.

When the three trainees got back, they kept all this to themselves, and said nothing to anyone. But Jesus' prayer had been answered, and he had the certainty he needed – his plan had come from the love of his Father; it was time to carry it through.

He came down the mountain to find a large crowd waiting.

'Teacher,' a man in the crowd cried out, 'please, please take pity on my son. He's my only child, and just look at him! An evil spirit gets hold of him. It suddenly shrieks and convulses him, and he foams at the mouth. It won't leave him alone, and it's destroying him. I begged your trainees to cast it out, but they couldn't.'

Jesus looked straight at his powerless, guilty-looking trainees, all still hooked on replacing the Romans. 'You disloyal, crooked lot,' Jesus blazed at them, 'you want to go down the same road as everyone else. How much longer have I got to put up with you?'

He turned to the man. 'Bring your son here to me,' Jesus said.

Even as he was bringing him, the 'demon' convulsed the boy. Jesus ordered it out, healed the child, and gave him back to his father. The whole crowd were awestruck, and thrilled with all he was doing. He turned to give his trainees a lesson on power.

'Let what the prophets say sink in,' he said, 'to rule, God's servant is sure to be handed over into the power of men.'

They never knew the prophets said that, and had no clue what they meant. But they didn't want to show their ignorance, and were too scared to ask him. Yet his unsettling talk raised the question of who was next in line as Number One. It started a heated argument.

Jesus saw what was going on, and stunned them. He took the least powerful person there, a little child, and stood the child next to himself.

'I give my authority to the one who accepts this child as my ambassador,' he told them, 'and only as you accept my authority, do you accept God's authority. The person who takes the role of your servant will be given the most power.'

The trainees couldn't understand this, and didn't believe it anyway. They were going to be the rulers. And they weren't going to let anyone else take their place.

'Master,' John said, 'We saw someone casting out demons in your name. He wasn't one of us, so we stopped him.'

'Don't stop him,' Jesus told them, 'anyone who isn't against you is on your side.'

They hadn't grasped a word he'd been saying. They had little time left to learn, and no idea what was about to happen to them.

PART FOUR: THE MARCH ON JERUSALEM

6 He sets out to reign in Jerusalem

[9.51-12.53]

Evil had lost the battle in the desert, but it still ruled Jerusalem. To do the job, Jesus must win through there. And there, evil held the tyrant's ultimate deterrent – death. If he tried to reign there, he'd die on a cross. He'd be lucky even to reach the city.

Armed with his strange time on the mountain, Jesus set himself to reign in Jerusalem. The Liberation Festival, the right time, was near. All his plans were now in place, though only his most trusted followers knew anything of them – and each only their own part.

He sent envoys ahead of him, and two told a Samaritan village to get ready. Samaritans, mixed-race semi-Jews, had their own Temple, and spurned Jerusalem. When they heard Jesus was going to Jerusalem, they refused to have him.

James and John were outraged.

'My lord,' they asked Jesus, 'shall we call down fire from heaven and wipe them out?' They were the servants of a new Elijah – and Elijah called down fire from heaven on his enemies! But Jesus turned his fire on them.

'Whose side are you on?' he demanded. 'My job is to save men from destruction, not destroy them.'

The two left quickly to find another village for the night.

And men kept coming to join him.

'I'll follow you anywhere,' one said.

'Foxes have holes, birds have nests,' Jesus told him, 'but God's servant has no place to rest outside Jerusalem.'

His march and 'place to rest' were not the sort the man was after.

'Follow me,' Jesus invited another man.

'I will,' he said, 'but I must see my father buried first.'

Being one of the Jewish family, he thought, was his ticket to God's government. But that out-dated idea would bring death to his family.

'Those who think God's rule is for the racial family,' Jesus replied, 'are as good as dead. They're going to be slaughtered. Let them bury their own dead. You go and spread the news of God government now.'

'I'll follow you, Master,' volunteered another, 'but I must get my family to agree.'

He too had the old idea of the racial family.

'If you look back to the old way,' Jesus told him, 'you're no use.'

Then Jesus copied Moses again, to give another sign of liberation. Moses chose seventy men to help him rule, so Jesus gave seventy his authority. He sent them in pairs, to every place on his route.

'Go for it,' he said, 'many are waiting. But watch out! I'm sending you like lambs in the midst of wolves, so keep moving. Before you stay at a house, offer it peace. If there's a peacemaker there, your peace will strengthen him. When a town welcomes you, tell them, "Share God's rule." If they accept you, they accept me – and my authority is God's.

'But if a place worships the land, say, "We shake off the dust of your idolatrous land – but don't forget, you had your chance to share in God's rule." Heaven help that place when the VRIN war starts. Its fate will be worse than Sodom's was. Ask them, "Do you think you can beat the Romans?" Tell them, "You'll be dead meat."'

When the seventy got back they were exploding with news of what happened.

'Sir,' they said, 'thanks to you we even got rid of demons!'

'Yes,' replied Jesus, 'I watched the devil fly like lightning to aid his minions. But nothing stopped you. I gave you authority to tread on snakes and scorpions, and overcome the enemy. But don't get high on that. Just be thrilled that you have a part in God's plan.'

Then Jesus revelled in the pure joy of the Spirit:

'Thank you Father, ruler of all, that a child can grasp what the cleverest failed to see. I thank you, Father, that this was your plan.'

Then he turned to his trainees.

'You're the lucky ones!' he said. 'You're seeing the arrival of God's rule on earth. Many prophets and rulers longed to see it, and never did.'

But the party was interrupted by a VRIN legal expert.

'Teacher,' he asked, 'you say, "those who do God's will, share his government." So what must I do?'

It was a trap. He wanted Jesus to say – as he had in Nazareth – that pagans might share God's government. That would soon put a stop to his march on Jerusalem.

'What does *The Law* say you must do?' Jesus said, throwing it back to trap the expert.

'First,' the expert answered, 'love the Lord your God with all your heart, soul, strength and mind. Second, love your neighbour as yourself.'

'Right,' said Jesus, 'so if you decide to do that, then you'll have a share in God's government.'

He'd called the expert's bluff. The expert wasn't doing that. He didn't love his Jewish neighbour, let alone foreigners.

'*The Law* tells us,' the expert replied, relaying the trap, 'that my fellow Jew is my neighbour. The question is, who else might be?'

The trap was open, but Jesus closed it on the expert:

> Robbers attacked a Jew going down from Jeru-
> salem. They took all he had, and left him for dead
> by the roadside. A Temple priest came along and
> saw him, but walked past on the other side. Then a
> Temple singer did the same.
>
> But when a Samaritan saw him, he went to him
> and bound up his wounds. He lifted him on his
> own pack animal, and took him to an inn. There he
> looked after him, and next day paid the man's bill.
> He told the host, 'Look after him. I'll pay what it
> costs you when I come back.'

'Which of them,' Jesus asked the expert, 'would you say was the Jew's neighbour?'

'The one with compassion,' he said, scorning the very word Samaritan.

The expert had sunk the VRIN view of God's government – rule from the Temple by the race. Because if the foreigner was the neighbour, those for the Temple were not!

'Make sure,' Jesus warned him, 'that you act on what you've said.'

For if he didn't, he'd end up 'by the roadside' – with no 'Samaritan' to save him from the Roman robbers.

And Jesus was upturning his view of women too, as a woman named Martha discovered. When she invited Jesus to her home, she found her sister, Mary, acting like a trainee. Mary was sitting at Jesus' feet learning to be a teacher – as if she was a man! In shock, Martha forgot herself. She too went into the men's quarter of the house.

'Sir,' she burst in, 'haven't you noticed? My sister has left me to serve on my own. Tell her to come into the women's quarter, and help with the work.'

'My dear Martha,' Jesus replied. 'You're upset, and worried about the work. But this is the crucial time. Only one thing is needed – to proclaim God's rule. Mary has chosen to do that, and no one's going to take that role from her.'

Some trainees weren't sure that God would give them victory when they reached Jerusalem. The next day one asked: 'My lord, will you teach us what to pray for? John taught his trainees how to pray.'

'When you pray,' Jesus replied, 'say:

> Father, liberate us; restore our true humanity; govern us now.

> Feed us and set your rule over all nations in Jerusalem.

> Forgive us the wrong all of us have done; for we forgive all who owe us anything.

> And spare us the terrible suffering needed to secure your victory.

But people had prayed for God's government for centuries, and God hadn't answered their prayers. So Jesus responded to the doubters.

'Suppose you have a friend,' he said. 'In the middle of the night you call to him, "My friend, lend me three loaves. A guest has arrived, and I've nothing to give him." His voice comes back, "We're all in bed and locked up. I can't get up now."

'He won't get up just because he's your friend. But if you keep on knocking, he'll get up and give you anything you want! I can tell you, God is better than any friend. If you ask him, he'll give you his rule. If you seek to be governed by him he'll guide you. If you knock, his door will open to all.

'Would any of you give your son a snake if he asks for a fish? Or a scorpion if he asks for an egg? Rotten fathers like you give only good things to your children. How much more will your heavenly Father govern and give you his holy Spirit. You have only to ask.'

But the trainees were worried about the Roman enemy. Jesus kept his mind on his enemy – evil, in any form. One day he freed a dumb man from the evil he suffered. The man began to talk, and the crowds were open-mouthed. But the VRIN saw a chance to attack him.

'Only the devil gives men magic power,' they murmured. 'The demon king gives him power over demons.'

'Do they think the demon king wants to get rid of his demons?' he asked the crowd. 'If so, like any government that fights itself, his will collapse.'

They said nothing.

'Your VRIN followers expel demons, don't they?' Jesus challenged them. 'If the demon king gives me power to drive out demons, how do your trainees do it? They should be warning you – you're headed for disaster.'

'Give us a sign,' one of them shouted.

'This healed man is a sign!' Jesus told him. 'Only God's power can deal with evil. This man was one of the lost tribes. If you won't welcome the lost tribes home, you're on evil's side. You'll exile everyone.

'The Hammerers showed us the way,' one of them shouted back.

'You celebrate the Hammerers,' Jesus replied, 'because they cleaned the Emperor's image from the Temple. But you VRIN make the Temple itself your image. That's seven times worse than what the Emperor did!'

This was too much for a VRIN woman in the crowd:

'How dare you say such things,' she shouted. 'You were born and bred in the Jewish family. God's government is for the Jewish family!'

'No,' he answered her. 'God's government is for those who listen to what God says and obey it.'

'If people want a sign, the only sign they'll get is one like the Ninevites got – a prophet warning of coming destruction! The Ninevites took the warning, and did a rethink. But with something far greater at stake, people today refuse to think.

'The VRIN want our nation resurrected to rule the world. I tell you the Empire of Nineveh will be resurrected before this generation!'

'The prophets say,' one of them barked back, 'we're the light for the nations.'

'Yes,' Jesus answered, 'to light the way for the nations. But you hide the light! If you were honest you'd see where you're headed. With twisted motives you're lost in the dark. Your 'light' is 'darkness'. You can't see you're bound for exile. If you were a 'light', the nations would want it.'

Then a local VRIN leader chose to tackle him. He invited him to a meal and Jesus went. But on arrival Jesus didn't do their ritual wash to mark him as a 'real' Jew. His host was shocked.

'You clean the outside just for appearance,' Jesus responded. 'Your dirty aim inside is to get the land for yourselves. You must be mad! Do you think God can't see what's going on inside you? Clean out your greed for the land and you'll really be clean.'

'But *The Law*,' his host countered, 'gives the land to us. We want God to rule our land, not the Romans. So we give a tenth of everything we have to the Temple, even of our herbs.'

'You want the land,' Jesus insisted. 'You're going to lose the Temple, because you don't obey the first commandment – "Love God." Do that and you can give the Temple a tenth of your mint sauce and the rest.'

'We're leading the way to God's government,' his host insisted, 'because we love God.'

'What you love,' Jesus replied, 'is being leaders. You like people to see you're important. What they can't see is that you're leading them to their death!'

'When you say that, you're insulting us too,' a legal expert burst out.

'Yes,' Jesus replied. 'And you legal experts are doing the same. You make strict laws, but don't lift a finger to help people be governed by God.'

'Then why,' the expert sniffed, 'do we build such fine tombs for the martyred prophets?'

'To celebrate your ancestors' success in killing them!' Jesus responded. 'This generation is going to suffer the consequences for the murder of every prophet. For all of them. From the beginning of time to your last victim – murdered at the altar in the Temple itself!'

'How can we be to blame?' the expert retorted.

'Because,' Jesus told him, 'you've made it impossible for people to know the truth. You've refused to accept God's rule yourselves, and you stop anyone else entering it.'

This stung. Their legal experts were out to get him from the moment Jesus left the house. They looked at anything he said to use against him. They had their spies watching him all the time, trying to find something.

Well aware of this, Jesus gave his trainees a strong warning.

'Don't be fooled by the VRIN,' he said. 'They're out to trap you. One day everyone will know what's going on. Take care what you tell them in private, because they will use it to destroy you. But friends, don't be scared of them. The worst they can do is kill you. What you need to be scared of is evil. It threatens to turn Jerusalem into a rubbish heap.

'But why are you so scared?' he asked them. 'Think of sparrows; they're two a penny. Yet God cares for each sparrow. Aren't you worth more than a sparrow? Throw your fears away. God cares for every hair on your head!'

Then he went on to speak of their future.

'After victory,' he said, 'if a man accepts me publicly, I accept him. Those rejecting me will die in the coming tragedy, but they can still do a rethink. Only if they reject the holy Spirit's way, are they sure to die fighting the Romans.

'People will charge you before community meetings, rulers, and authorities,' he said. 'Don't worry. The holy Spirit will tell you how to answer.'

The crowds round him now were huge. People were trampling on each other. One man shouted out:

'Teacher, tell my brother to give me my share of the family land.'

'Tell me, sir,' Jesus answered, 'who made me your judge?

'At all costs,' he told the crowd, 'guard against greed for the land. The resurrection has nothing to do with the land you own.

> A rich man's land grew such huge crops he couldn't store it all. He thought, 'I'll pull down my barns and build bigger.'
>
> He told himself, 'Now you're secure for years, enjoy the good life!' But God said to him, 'You fool, tonight you die. So who'll get it all?'

The answer, of course, was the Romans. War could start at any time, and the man would die fighting for his land.

'That'll happen to you,' Jesus told them, 'if you think having land will get you God's government.'

And he kept warning his trainees, they must be ready to lose the land. But they thought if they lost their land, they'd have no food.

'Idolaters live to eat and get things,' Jesus told them. 'Life under God's control is much more than that. So don't worry about losing the land. Look at the crows. They don't sow crops, yet God feeds them. Aren't you worth more than birds? Can worry make you grow taller? If it can't even do that, what use is it?

'Flowers don't worry about clothes. Yet even Solomon in all his finery couldn't match one of them. If God gives clothes to weeds, won't he clothe his envoys? You don't trust God at all. Your Father does know you need these things. Be governed by him, and all your needs will be met.

'Don't be scared of anyone,' Jesus added, 'your Father has chosen to give you – few that you are – his government. So sell your land, and give the money to those in need. Put your security in living under God's control. Nothing devalues there and thieves can't get at it. What you do with your land will show what you really live for.'

Then he gave them Moses' watchword on the first Liberation night:

'Be dressed for action!' he told them. 'Be like servants ready to open the door the moment their lord returns. Their lord will prepare everything, have them sit down to eat, and come and serve them.'

That made no sense to them. Yes, God, the Lord, was returning to Jerusalem, and they must be ready. But lords didn't serve! Jesus' words sounded as if God would lose and be made a slave! And Jesus added again the terrible warning he kept giving them:

'The VRIN should have known the consequence of making the Temple their idol. It's certain to be destroyed, but no one knows just when. You must be ready for it the moment you hear the Romans are coming.'

'Master,' Peter cut in, keen to mark that he would be in charge. 'Is this just for us, or do we tell everyone?'

'It's for the one in charge,' the Master answered. 'The one in charge serves the rest. If he acts like an idolater, the Romans will arrive when he's drunk. They'll cut him to pieces with the rest.'

The trainees were baffled. They were thinking of victory, and ruling a resurrected nation.

'Do you think it's my job,' Jesus asked them, 'to get the land for the Jewish family? No! It's to face people with their choice: rethink or die. It's to set fire to their idolatry – and I must go through the fire myself to do it. I can't wait for it to be over! Until the job's done, the pressure's just too much.'

But the VRIN were circling, to stop him even reaching Jerusalem.

7 They fail to turn him back

[12.54-14.35]

Jesus pressed on, addressing the crowds: 'You can read the signs of the weather – a cloud from the west means rain, a south wind means a heat wave – so why can't you read the signs that God's government is here? It's because you only pretend you want it. What you really want is to get rid of the Romans.

'Don't get into a small dispute with a Roman,' he warned them. 'Make peace with the man. If you don't, your small dispute will grow, and spark an all-out war. When that war starts, God's judgement won't fall on the Romans, it'll fall on you. You'll lose everything.'

The VRIN's answer was an attempt to abort his journey. They brought him dire news from Jerusalem. A gang of northerners had gone to the Temple to sacrifice. Roman Governor Pilate had got wind of an uprising, sent in troops and slaughtered the lot. The soldiers mixed the northerners' blood with their sacrifices.

Everyone was horrified. Surely, it was now too dangerous for Jesus to go there? But Jesus detected evil seeking to turn him back.

'Do you think,' he asked them, 'that these northerners were worse than other northerners? Not one bit. Roman swords will slaughter them all, unless they rethink their policy.

'The same goes for southerners. When the tower of Siloam fell down, were the eighteen crushed worse than others in Jerusalem? Not one bit! Unless Jerusalem rethinks its policy, siege engines will bring down all their buildings on top of them.'

'This generation,' he told them, 'has one last chance to avoid that fate. If it doesn't produce light for the nations now, it's done for. Like a barren fig tree, the owner will say to the gardener, "Cut it down."' And the gardener would be the Romans. Jesus was offering a last chance to avoid that fate.

On the holy day he taught in the meeting place. A woman there was bent double. For eighteen years she'd been unable to stand up straight. When Jesus saw her, he called her to him.

'Woman,' he said, laying his hands on her, 'you are freed from the evil you suffer.'

She stood up straight, and began thanking God, but the VRIN leader of the meeting was furious.

'*The Law* says,' the leader fumed, 'there are six days for doing work. Come on one of those days to be cured. No work must be done on the holy day.'

But the leader had forgotten what *The Law* also said – the holy day was a sign for their liberation!

'You VRIN are hypocrites,' Jesus responded, 'claiming to lead the people to freedom. You untie and set free your donkey on the holy day, to let it drink. Why shouldn't this woman be freed from the evil that's tied her down for eighteen years? *The Law* says the holy day is for celebrating liberation. I'm obeying it. You're breaking it – trying to keep a woman in slavery on the holy day!'

Jesus' words were a knock-out and the crowd were thrilled. So Jesus asked the leader:

'What is God's government like? What can you compare it to?'

Getting no reply, he gave the answer: 'It's like a mustard seed that a man sowed in his field. It grew into a great tree.'

The leader agreed. The prophet said it was a seed, set to become the greatest tree on earth. The leader imagined that the VRIN were the seed. But Jesus concluded:

'Birds came from everywhere to make their home in its branches.'

The leader couldn't tell who the 'birds' were. Were they Jews coming home from exile – or were they the nations coming to make their home in God's government? And Jesus added another puzzle for him.

'How do you see God's government?' Jesus asked him again.

Again he got no reply. 'It's like yeast,' Jesus said, 'which a woman hid in bowl of flour. You couldn't see it, but the whole lot rose up.'

God's rule was hidden from the leader. He couldn't see it rising up all round him. Jesus left him, and went on with his journey. But even his own trainees were expecting victory over the Romans.

'Sir,' one follower wondered, 'will only a few of us survive the victory?'

'You won't get through the door into God's government with all your baggage,' Jesus told him. 'You're headed for destruction with the VRIN. You'll only wake up when it's too late. When the Romans arrive it'll be no use saying, "We agreed with him really." With bitter tears you'll see people from north, south, east and west given your place. You people will be the last to accept God as your ruler.'

Then some of the VRIN made another attempt to abort his journey.'Get away,' they told him, 'out of the country. Herod is looking for you to kill you.'

'Then I must certainly keep going,' Jesus replied. 'It wouldn't do for a prophet to be killed anywhere except Jerusalem. You can tell that fox Herod that I'm busy today and tomorrow, tackling evil and healing. But on the third day I shall complete my work in Jerusalem.

'Oh Jerusalem, Jerusalem,' he groaned, 'killer of the prophets and lynch-mob of those sent to you. How I've longed to save your children from the approaching fire, but you refuse to let me. So watch out! Your Temple is now godless, left to the fire to engulf it.'

'Who do you think you are?' said the VRIN.

'You won't know that,' he answered, 'till you join me to proclaim God's government on earth.'

Then a national leader of the VRIN decided to invite Jesus to a meal. It was the holy day, and on the way there Jesus met a man suffering from dropsy. 'Is it lawful,' Jesus asked the VRIN shadowing him, 'to heal on the holy day or not?'

It was a crunch question. If God's rule was back the answer was yes. No one replied, so Jesus healed him and set him free. That showed that the day of liberation had come, but his shadowers didn't look pleased.

'Suppose your son,' Jesus said, 'fell into a well on the holy day. Wouldn't you pull him out? So won't God rescue his children?'

He wasn't one of God's children, they thought – but didn't say . . .

As Jesus arrived, he watched all the VRIN go for seats at the top table. When more important guests arrived, they had to give them up. So he announced to everyone:

> Don't go for the top seats in God's government, or you'll be humiliated. The host will say, 'Give your seat to someone more important' – and you won't get a seat!
>
> If you want to be at the top in God's government, take the lowest place. Then he'll let you share the glory of those at his top table.
>
> If you think you're the most important, you'll be the last person to enter God's government. The way in is to act as the servant.

This brought a sharp reaction from one of the VRIN there. He thought Jesus was inviting all the wrong people.

'We'll be the ones invited to that glorious feast,' he asserted. 'It's for real Jews like us.'

'But you don't come to the glorious feast when you're invited,' Jesus answered. Then he told them all:

> A man invited guests to the glorious feast. He sent his servant to tell the guests, 'The meal is served.' But the first man invited said, 'I'm getting some land, excuse me.' The next said, 'I've bought ten oxen and must plough my land.' Another said, 'I've just got married, and the family comes first.'

> The host was furious. He told his servant, 'Quick! Go into the streets and alleys of the town. Bring in the poor, the handicapped, the blind, and the lame.'

> The servant obeyed and reported back, 'Sir, I've done what you said, and there's still room.'

> 'Then go out of town,' the master told him, 'to the highways and hedgerows. Compel people to come in. See to it that my house is full.' Then he added, 'Not one of those invited will get any of my feast.'

Jesus left the national leader and his guests to ponder who those 'outside the town' might be. He left to resume his journey with the crowds flocking around him. He gave them the same warning: don't worship the land and family; it will bring your destruction.

'God's rule is not based on race,' he kept telling them. 'If you think it is, you're not my follower. Those going my way want nothing for themselves. My way is through the cross, the only way to see God govern.

'But if you think like the VRIN,' he told them, 'you'll have to pay for it. Hoping to beat the Romans is building castles in the air:

> Before a man builds a tower, he makes sure that he's got the resources to do it. If he starts to build and then goes broke, he's a laughing stock. People will say, 'That's the man who started building and couldn't finish.'

Then he cut the VRIN even nearer to the bone:

> Does any ruler start a war without first weighing the odds? If he's only got ten thousand men, he thinks, 'I can't defeat a ruler with twice as many.' So while the other ruler is still far off, he agrees to any peace terms.

But the VRIN weren't listening. The land was going to be lost, and Jesus kept telling people: 'If you haven't said good-bye to your land, you can't be one of my trainees.'

And the land was going, because they weren't doing their job.

'Our people,' he said, 'were called to be salt, to cleanse and heal the nations. But what use is salt that isn't salty? It's no use for the land – or the dung heap – it's thrown out. Let those who get the message take it in!'

Unable to stop his advance to Jerusalem, the VRIN reaction was nasty.

8 He gives them their choice

[15.1-16.31]

Suddenly there was a whispering campaign. 'He thinks God's government is for tax collectors,' the VRIN murmured, 'and sex-workers! He goes running to welcome non-Jews as our people!'

Jesus answered that these people were the lost tribes. He was welcoming the exiles home. His reply was a volley of stories. Coding himself as shepherd and the lost tribes as lost sheep, he began:

> If a shepherd has a hundred sheep and loses one, what does he do? He leaves the ninety-nine and looks for the lost one. When he finds it, he'll invite his friends and neighbours in to celebrate.

> I promise you, when anyone does a rethink there's a huge celebration to welcome him. But the ninety-nine VRIN are sure they're right. They refuse to rethink, so miss the party.

So the VRIN were hypocrites, he claimed, saying they wanted to end the exile. In fact they were trying to stop the exiles' return – in the way an elder son treated his exiled brother:

> A man had two sons. The younger wished his father was dead, so he could get his land. He said, 'Father, give me now the land I'm going to inherit.' So the father divided his land between them. The younger son's conduct forced him out of the village. He sold his share, and went into exile far away, where he spent his money having fun.

> When his money ran out, there was a severe famine. The only job he could get was feeding pigs. He would have eaten the pigs' food if only he could.

Nobody gave him a thing, and to stay alive he had to steal.

The crowd knew that he was telling their story. Their ancestors had gone after man-made gods, and wished their 'Father' were dead. That was why they were still exiled from him, ruled by idolaters. They waited, eager to hear how their exile would end:

Then he thought, 'my father's workers have more than enough to eat, while I'm dying of hunger. I'll go home and say, "Father, I've done wrong, and I don't deserve to be your son. Will you take me on as one of your paid workers?"' So he set off back to his father.

When his father saw him in the distance, he was overwhelmed with compassion for him. As he ran to hug him, the son said, 'Father, I've sinned against God and wronged you. I don't deserve to be your son.'

But the father was already calling his servants, 'Hurry! Get the royal robe and put it on him! Put the royal ring on his finger, and royal sandals on his feet! Bring the prime beef calf, it's time for the feast. My son was dead, and he's resurrected. He was lost, and his exile's ended.' And the feast got going.

The crowd were elated. God's government 'feast' was arriving! The end of their exile was at hand. But, suddenly, Jesus said, there was a problem.

The elder son out in the fields heard the music and dancing. He asked one of the servants what was going on. He was told, 'Your brother's come home, and your father's killed the prime beef calf to celebrate.'

The older brother reacted with fury, and refused to go in. When his father came out to plead with him, he fumed at his father.

> 'Look here! I've been slaving for you all these
> years, and never disobeyed a single order. But
> you've never given me even a little goat for a party
> with my friends. This son of yours has swallowed
> up all your property with sex workers. Yet when he
> comes home you kill the prime beef calf for him!'

Of course the elder son was lying. The property
was his – his father had already given it to him.
Now, he was trying to disown his own brother.
Worst of all, he was abusing his father. His con-
duct was more outrageous than his brother's had
been:

> The father said to him, 'Son, you're always with
> me, and all the property is yours. But we had to
> celebrate, because your own brother was dead and is
> resurrected. Your own brother was lost and has been
> found.'

And there the story stopped – half-way
through. Would the VRIN, the elder brother, now
decide to welcome the exiles home? If they didn't
and kept God's government to themselves, they'd
be treated like a common embezzler. Jesus warned
what would happen to them:

> A rich man employed a manager, only to find
> that the man was embezzling his goods. He called
> the man in and said, 'What's this I hear about you?
> Get your accounts in order. You're fired.'

> The man had to think fast, 'What can I do? I'm
> about to lose my job. I'm not fit for manual work,
> and I can't face begging.' Then he thought, 'I'll fix it
> so that after I leave here I'll be looked after.'

> So he called in all his employer's debtors.
> He asked the first, 'How much do you owe my
> employer?'

'A hundred barrels of olive oil,' the man answered.

The manager told him, 'Here's your bill. Quick, change it to fifty.' Then he asked another, 'How much do you owe?'

'A hundred containers of wheat,' he replied.

'Here's your bill,' he told him, 'make it eighty.'

'You've got to give that crook some credit,' Jesus said. 'At least he used his brains and did something about it, when his job was going. That's more than you can say for the VRIN. They're about to lose their job, but refuse to use their brains to rethink.'

'Keep well away from him,' the VRIN retaliated, 'that's our advice.'

'And my advice,' Jesus responded, 'is to choose friends who haven't made the land their god. Then, after the land's been lost, you'll still have friends to welcome you into God's government.'

'We can't lose the land,' the VRIN retorted. '*The Law* tells us that God will entrust the whole earth to us!'

'God gave you a little land,' Jesus responded, 'and you've made it your god. Yet you think God will trust you with the whole earth? Didn't they tell you, "Those who are honest with a little, can be trusted with a lot. Those corrupt with a little will be corrupt with a lot."'

'We are God's real servants,' the VRIN replied.

'No servant can serve two masters,' Jesus insisted. 'You worship the land. You can't serve God and the gods of materialism.'

'We want God's government,' protested the VRIN.

'You say that,' Jesus replied, 'but God sees your real aim – to get control of the land.'

'But *The Law*,' they countered, 'promised us the land.'

'*The Law* was given,' Jesus reminded them, 'until God's rule was in place. Since John came, God's rule is arriving, but you want a war to get it. *The Law*'s judgement falls on those serving man-made gods.'

He had now reached the spot where John had condemned Herod for stealing Herodias, his brother's wife. So the VRIN tried to trap Jesus into condemning Herod. Herodias had forced Herod's brother to divorce her, so they asked Jesus about divorce. But Jesus turned the tables on them.

'Moses allowed divorce,' Jesus said, 'because God's command – do not commit adultery – was too difficult for them. But under God's rule, people are given a new heart and are transformed. Divorce is no longer needed. A man who divorces his wife to marry another, or marries a divorced woman, then would commit adultery. Do you want to go on in the old way, stealing other men's wives – like Herod?'

Being classed with Herod ended the argument, so again he warned where they were headed. He told an old well known story, putting a new sting in it:

A rich man hated a poor, sick, man, named Lazarus, lying at his gate. When Lazarus died, he joined Abraham, awaiting the resurrection. At his death, the rich man found himself in anguish. He saw Lazarus with Abraham, and cried, 'Father Abraham, help! Send Lazarus to dip the tip of his finger in water to cool my tongue. I'm in torment in these flames.'

'Child,' Abraham replied, 'you got the land, while Lazarus was a victim of your policy. Now he's waiting for the resurrection, while you face the consequences. It's too late now.'

'Then, father,' the man cried, 'send Lazarus to warn my VRIN brothers. I don't want them to end up in this terrible agony.'

'They have *The Law* and *The Prophets*,' Abraham told him. "They warn them of the consequence of serving man-made gods. They must listen to them."

'They aren't listening, father Abraham,' the man pleaded. 'But if someone goes to them from the dead, they'll change their policy.'

'If they won't listen to Moses,' Abraham replied, 'they won't listen to anyone rising from the dead.'

People were 'rising from the dead' all around them – resurrected as real Jews – and they couldn't see them. One more would make no difference.

9 He prepares his men for the assault

[17.1-19.10]

His own trainees were full of VRIN ideas. 'You're bound to be tempted to go the VRIN's way at times,' Jesus said. 'Don't bring that fate on anyone. Being thrown in the sea with a rock round your neck is better than that. But if one of you falls for their line, warn him where he's going. If he does a rethink, forgive him – seven times a day if you have to.'

But some of the trainees were wondering whether Jesus was going to win.

'Give us more grounds, Master,' they asked, 'to increase our trust in you.'

'Trust?' the Master queried. 'You don't trust me at all. If you did, you could tell this mulberry tree to jump in the sea, and it would.

'What right have you,' he fired at their arrogance, 'to make demands? If your slave came in from ploughing, would you say, "Take a break and have your dinner"? Wouldn't you say, "Get my dinner ready; then serve me while I eat it. When you've done everything, you can have yours."

'Would you thank a slave for doing what he was told? So when you've done everything, tell yourselves, "We slaves are a dead loss. At best we've only done what we were ordered."'

With that he moved on, travelling through the border region with Samaria. There a group of ten lepers saw him.

'Jesus! Master!' the lepers shouted, 'have pity on us!'

'Go and show yourselves to the priests,' Jesus told them – and as they went, they were healed.

Like a good Jew, one came back to thank Jesus, yelling, 'Praise God!' – for the word 'Jew' means 'a-praise-God-man' – but the man praising God was a Samaritan.

'Weren't ten healed?' Jesus asked him. 'Where are the other nine? Weren't any of them 'praise-God-men', except this Samaritan?

'Join in the resurrection,' Jesus said to him. 'Your trust in me has won you a share in God's rule.'

The VRIN boiled over.

'Don't you know,' they snapped, 'that the Emperor still rules us? You tell us God's government is arriving: when are we going to see it?'

'The way you're looking,' Jesus replied, 'you won't ever see it. You'll never say, "We've set up God's government here," or anywhere. Open your eyes. God's rule is yours to accept now.'

But his trainees too were still hoping for liberation from the Romans. So again he began trying to tell them:

'God's servant must first be rejected by this idolatrous generation. He must suffer a time of terrible anguish, before he's vindicated. So don't be taken in by the VRIN when they say: "It's judgement day for idolaters." On that day they'll be the idolaters who are destroyed – and the whole world will know about it!

'It'll take them by surprise,' he added, 'just as the flood surprised people in Noah's day. Roman armies will flood in, and drown this generation. Then everyone will know whether I'm telling the truth or the VRIN are. You'll know that day has arrived, when you hear the Roman armies are coming. Get away at once! Don't go back into your house to get anything.'

'Master,' the puzzled trainees asked him, 'Where will this happen?'

'Where there's any revolt,' Jesus replied. 'The Romans will gather like vultures, and they'll be doomed.'

This scene was his trainees' worst nightmare. To spur them to keep going, he told a story:

> There was a judge with no fear of God or respect for anyone. A widow kept coming to beg him, 'Give me justice against my enemy.' For a long time he wouldn't, but in the end he thought, 'I don't fear God or respect anyone, but this widow is causing me a problem. I'd better grant her justice, or she may do me an injury.'

'Think of that,' Jesus said, 'even a corrupt judge gave a woman justice because she kept on and on at him. Won't God give his own people what he's planned for them, when they plead day and night? Do you think God wants to delay?

But when he gives his verdict, will any of you be found faithful to me?'

And again he made their choice clear:

Two men went to the Temple to pray, one a VRIN, the other a tax collector. The VRIN stood at the front. 'God,' he said, 'I thank you I'm a real Jew, not like that tax collector and others. I fast twice a week to pray for liberation. I give a tenth of my income to our national cause at the Temple.'

But the tax collector stood at the back, and hung his head. 'God, forgive me,' he said, 'I've been going the wrong way.'

'The man doing the rethink,' Jesus said, 'will be the one governed by God. The VRIN think they're going to be the rulers – under God – but those who think they're the most important will lose everything. Those they think are least important, are the most important.'

But the trainees wanted to get the important people on their side. When mothers brought toddlers for him to touch, they stopped them. No one thought infants were important. But Jesus jumped on the trainees.

'Let them come,' he ordered them. 'I'm telling the truth: it's the least important who receive God's authority. If you don't think you're the least important, you can't be one of God's executives.'

Then a man the trainees thought most important came up – a big landowner from the ruling party.

'Good Teacher,' he asked Jesus, 'what must I do to obtain a share in the new age?'

'Why do you call me good?' Jesus answered. 'Only God is good. Obey the commandments:

don't commit adultery; don't murder; don't steal; don't lie; honour your father and mother.'

'I have kept them all,' the man replied, 'ever since I was a boy.'

Jesus saw that the man was serious.

'There's still one thing you need to do,' Jesus told him. 'Sell all your land. Give the money to those in need, and you'll share the riches of God's rule. Then come and follow me.'

When he heard that the man's face fell, because his hopes were tied to his land.

'You can't enter the new age,' Jesus told him, 'and keep your land.'

Jesus watched him go, and foresaw his fate. He would die trying to defend his land.

'It's impossible for a big landowner to accept God's rule,' Jesus told the trainees. 'A camel will go through the eye of a needle first.'

'What!' exclaimed the trainees. 'Then what chance has anyone got?'

'Things people can't do,' Jesus replied, 'God can.'

But Peter was hoping to become quite a landowner himself.

'Yes,' he said, 'but what are we going to get out of this? We've left all we've got to follow you.'

'If you've let go your family and land rights for God's rule,' Jesus replied, 'you'll get oceans more – of family and land, both now and in the coming age.'

'But get this straight,' he told them. 'All the prophets said about God's servant will happen at Jerusalem. He'll be handed over to the Romans, ridiculed, humiliated and spat on. After they've flogged him, they'll kill him, and on the third day he'll rise again.'

This, the trainees assumed, was more tough talk. If he was going to rise, he would triumph. And their hopes grew stronger with all he did. As he reached the last town before Jerusalem, a blind beggar was sat by the roadside. The man heard the crowd going by, and wanted to know what was happening.

'It's Jesus of Nazareth coming through,' someone told him.

'Jesus! Son of David!' the man shouted. 'Have pity on me!'

Those going in front of Jesus told the man to shut up – Jesus had given strict orders not to use such language.

'Son of David!' the man yelled even louder, 'have pity on me!'

Jesus stopped, and ordered the man to be brought to him.

'What do you want me to do for you?' Jesus asked.

'My lord,' the man said, 'let me see again.'

All the crowd behind had their eyes fixed on the man.

'Receive your sight,' Jesus said. 'Your trust in me has won you a share in the victory.'

At once the man could see. He followed Jesus praising God, and the whole crowd joined with him. As he entered the town a small man named Zacchaeus wanted to see him. He was a wealthy chief tax collector, and couldn't get near because of the crowd. So he ran ahead and climbed a sycamore tree.

When Jesus reached the spot, he looked up and saw him.

'Zacchaeus,' he called, 'quick! Come down. I must stay at your house today.'

Zacchaeus climbed down as fast as he could, overjoyed. But the crowd were shocked.

'He's going to stay,' hissed the VRIN, 'at a filthy traitor's house.'

But Zacchaeus faced the crowd, and pledged himself to Jesus.

'Sir,' he said, 'I'll give half of all I've got to the poor. If I've taken anything from anyone dishonestly, I'll give them back four times as much.'

People couldn't believe their ears.

'Today,' Jesus announced, 'liberation has reached this man's house. He's now a returned exile. My work is to find and bring back victorious the lost tribes!'

But such talk risked wrecking his whole plan.

PART FIVE: THE RULER'S VICTORY AND REIGN

10 The ruler storms the city

[19.11-48]

They were about to start on the road up to the city itself. His talk of victory overexcited his trainees. It gave them ideas of becoming the rulers by nightfall! They needed a cold dip in reality, and he gave it them. He used the story of old Herod's son, First-of-the-people.

On old Herod's death his son First-of-the-people had sped to Rome to be made ruler. A delegation of leading Jews quickly followed, to dissuade the Emperor. But they failed, and First-of-the-people returned to Jerusalem as ruler. His first act was to have the whole delegation slaughtered in front of him. Jesus began:

> A prince went off to ask the Emperor to make him ruler. Before he left, he gave a piece of gold to each of his ten servants. He said, 'Trade with these till I return.' But his fellow citizens hated him. They sent a delegation after him to tell the Emperor that they didn't want him as their ruler.

> When the prince returned as ruler, he called in his servants to judge what they'd done. The first said, 'My lord, I've made ten times as much.'

> 'Well done!' said the ruler. 'You proved trustworthy with a small amount, so take charge of ten cities.'

> The second said, 'My lord, I've made five times as much.'

> And the ruler said, 'Take charge of five cities.'
>
> Then a third said, 'My lord, here's your money. I kept it safe in a handkerchief. I was afraid, because you're a hard man. You profit where you don't invest, and reap what you don't sow.'
>
> 'You worthless slave!' said the ruler. 'You've condemned yourself. You knew what I was like, so why didn't you put my money in the bank? It would have gained some interest on my return.'
>
> 'Take the money from him,' he ordered his aides. 'Give it to the one who made most. Everyone who's got it will be given more. But anyone who hasn't got it is going to lose all he's got!'
>
> Then the ruler said, 'Bring here these enemies of mine, who wouldn't have me as their ruler. Slaughter them in front of me.'

And the trainees still hadn't 'got it'. Unless they got what he was saying, they would share the fate of those rejecting him. But they'd got enough to know that those slaughtered were not Romans, but Jews. The trainees hit the ground with a bump, and Jesus was ready to go. He strode ahead up the winding road from Jericho, to rule in Jerusalem.

To complete his work, he had five outstanding tasks to finish there. He had to:

- publicly defeat his people's enemy

- deliver God's judgement on the Temple and city

- sign the promised new contract to renew creation

- lay the foundation stone of a new Temple

- establish God's government on earth for ever

As he neared the city, his secret preparations came to light. The villages of Bethphage and Bethany came into view, and he called two trainees to him.

'Go into the village over there,' he told them. 'As you enter it you'll find a young donkey tethered, untie it and bring it here. If anyone asks, "Why are you untying it?" give them the password, "Because its master needs it."'

The two went off and found the young donkey where he'd said. They began to untie it.

'Why are you untying it?' the owners asked.

'Because,' they replied giving the password, 'its master needs it.'

With that, the two of them took the donkey. They threw their cloaks on its back and lifted Jesus on to it. As he rode along, people spread their cloaks on the road. When the path started to go down from the Mount of Olives, the crowd began to celebrate. They praised God for all his power that they'd seen in action. They shouted the words of the prophet at the top of their voices:

> 'Your ruler comes to you riding on a donkey's foal.'

Then they began singing the triumphal Festival song:

> 'Hail to the ruler who comes in the name of the Lord! He brings peace and the victory of God!'

'Teacher,' some VRIN yelled from the crowd, 'tell your trainees to shut up.'

'If they do,' he answered, 'the prophet said the stones themselves will start shouting!'

As Jesus approached the city, he looked straight at it. Foreseeing the appalling horror it was bringing on itself, tears flooded down his cheeks. Like the prophet of old he pronounced its coming destruction.

'If only you could see...' he wept, broken-hearted, 'even you... what you're now being offered... but you refuse to see it, and you've sealed your fate. Your enemies will surround you, barricade you in, and blockade you in every direction. Their siege engines will bring your buildings crashing down onto your children. They won't leave a stone standing, because you failed to recognise the time of God's return.'

He entered the city, and went into the Temple courtyard. There he halted the sale of sacrificial animals. No sacrificial animals meant no sacrifices, and no sacrifices meant there was no Temple. The ruler had symbolically demolished it – and the ruler alone could rebuild it.

'The prophet says,' Jesus reminded them,

My House is to be a House of prayer...

He paused, for the prophet's next words were explosive: *for all nations.* Leaving the words unsaid, he concluded instead with the verdict of another prophet on the Temple:

You have made it a hideout for terrorists.

It was a direct challenge to the entire Jewish establishment. The priestly rulers had watched

his activities, with puzzled and growing concern.
Now, he was blatantly acting as ruler of the Jews.
But the Jewish authorities were stuck, for the man
was the people's hero of the hour.

He'd neither done nor said anything violent to
warrant arrest. And to arrest him in the crowds
might cause a riot. That would doubly undermine
their authority – Governor Pilate would blame
them for the riot, while the crowds would see
them as Roman puppets.

At dusk Jesus disappeared in the crowds, to
a safe place outside the city. And when morning
came the next day, the authorities found him back
teaching in the Temple. The crowds were again
hanging on his every word. Again at night he
vanished, and each day it was the same. All that
the chief priests, legal experts, and Jewish lords
could do was to watch and wait.

The Roman guards on duty at the Temple
showed not the slightest interest in the man. He
was causing no disturbance, and was no threat
to Rome. He was just another Jew. If there was a
problem it was a purely Jewish matter. Rome was
above such things.

11 The establishment's resistance is futile

[20.1-21.38]

As the Festival day approached, the authorities' fears increased. The growing crowds Jesus was drawing threatened their control. Unless they acted, they could lose control. So they sent an imposing party to trap him. Their aim was to get him to state that he was the ruler. If he did that, then Rome would have to act.

'Why,' they began, 'are you acting in this way? May we know what authority you have, and where you get it from?'

No ruler announces himself. It is the citizen's duty to hail him. The people had done this on his entry to the city. His display of authority at the Temple required the chief priests and lords to do the same. So his response reversed their question.

'I've a question,' he replied, 'for you. Tell me, was John the prophet sent by God to precede the ruler's arrival? Or was he a false prophet?'

They were caught. They turned to discuss among themselves how to answer: 'We daren't say John was a fraud, or the crowds will stone us. They're convinced he was a prophet. But if we admit that John was the forerunner, we'll have to say he's the ruler!'

So they said, 'we can't tell where John's authority came from.'

'Then nor can I tell you,' Jesus replied, 'where my authority comes from.'

Up to this moment his stories had all been in code – so the establishment wouldn't understand – but now he told a story in open code, which everybody knew. Turning to the people, he began:

> A man planted a vineyard, leased it to tenants, and went abroad. When the harvest came, he sent a servant to collect the rent. But the tenants beat the servant and sent him back with nothing. So the owner sent another servant, and they treated him the same way. When the owner sent a third, they beat him up and threw him out too. 'What can I do?' the owner of the vineyard said.

Everyone knew he was telling the authorities' the story of how they rejected all the prophets. God was the owner, the people the vineyard, the rulers the tenants, and the prophets the servants. But Jesus was about to give them the story's ending:

> 'I'll send my beloved son,' the owner said. 'Surely they'll respect him.' But when the tenants saw the son they said, 'This is the heir – let's kill him. Then we can claim the vineyard for ourselves.' So they took him out of the vineyard and killed him.
>
> Now what do you think the owner of the vineyard will do to them? He'll come and wipe out those tenants, and give the vineyard to others.

The crowd was aghast. Surely they wouldn't reject the promised ruler, the son of God! He was to bring God's rule on earth.

'God forbid!' they all cried out.

'Then why,' Jesus asked, 'does the prophet tell us, "The stone that the builders rejected is the foundation stone"?'

For the prophet had warned that if they rejected the foundation stone:

> Everyone who trips over that stone will be broken into pieces. Anyone it falls on will be ground into the dust.

The authorities had no answer, and left humiliated. So they decided to try again, and used agents acting like VRIN. These put the crunch question to him – the Emperor's tax. Since the big rebellion twenty years earlier, it had been the vital issue.

'Teacher,' they shouted from the crowd, 'we agree with you. You're not scared of the Emperor! You give an honest answer to every question. Is it right that we should pay tax to the Emperor?'

If he said yes, they knew his support from the crowds would vanish. And if he said no, the Romans would finish him. The trap was clear, but Jesus saw through the trappers.

'Show me a tax coin,' he demanded, 'and I'll tell you what you can do with it!'

No true VRIN would even look at the coin. It bore the image of the Emperor and blasphemous text, 'the son of god'. Yet the trappers held up the graven image in the Temple itself! Two hundred years earlier that act had started the Hammerers' war of liberation.

'This image,' Jesus asked, milking the moment to the full, 'and this writing. Who do they belong to?'

The crowd loved it. He was pretending not even to recognise the coin.

'The Emperor,' the trappers mumbled, nakedly exposed as establishment stooges.

'Then,' said Jesus, using the words that launched the Hammerers' liberation struggle, '"pay the Emperor back what he deserves…"'

No one could argue with that! But taxes, Jesus said, weren't their problem. And he completed the old Hammerer's last words hammering the real issue, idolatry. Let them end their idolatrous abuse of God's Temple:

'…and give the Temple that belongs to God, back to him.'

The trappers quickly disappeared.

But some wealthy lords decided to tackle him. He was talking about resurrection. That was VRIN-speak for revolution – resurrecting the Jewish state – with their martyred freedom-fighters bodily resurrected to share it. The books of *The Prophets*, they claimed, taught them this.

But the authorities accepted only the books of *The Law*. They found no talk of resurrection there. Everyone knew, they said, that dead bodies stay dead. The very idea of resurrection was a joke. They had an old tale to make it a laughing stock, and came to try it on Jesus.

'Teacher,' they began, 'if a man's brother dies leaving a wife but no children, Moses decrees,

> The man must marry the widow and raise children for his brother.

'Well, there were seven brothers. The first married and died childless, so the second married the widow. When he died the third married her. In the same way all seven married her, and all died childless. Finally the woman died. So in this resurrection, whose wife will the woman be? All seven married her.'

'Moses made that rule,' Jesus responded, 'because people marry to secure land and family rights. But there are no such rights in the age to come. Those resurrected are not the racial family. They're those who act like sons and do the Father's will. They don't marry and die, but live forever – as angels do.'

And then Jesus added a knock-out. 'Don't you know,' he asked, 'that *The Law* of Moses tells us of the resurrection? At the time of the people's resurrection from Egypt, God told Moses:

> I am the God of Abraham, Isaac, and Jacob.

If God is their God, they must be alive waiting for the final resurrection. Everyone is alive to him. God isn't a god of the dead, but the God of the living.'

Even the VRIN liked that one.

'A good answer, teacher,' everyone cheered.

And after that reply the legal experts didn't dare to put any further questions. So Jesus put a question to them.

'The legal authorities admit that the promised ruler is David's son. So how can they refuse to recognise him as their lord? David himself called his promised descendant his lord:

> God said to my lord [his son! the promised ruler]: 'Sit at my right hand until I make your enemies your footstool.'

'We know that a father is always lord over his son. If even David calls the promised ruler his lord, how can the authorities fail to do so? David indeed foresaw that his son would be:

> supreme priest over all High Priests forever.

The legal experts had no answer. Those made his 'footstool' meant they would be destroyed. And Jesus gave his last words of warning about these legal experts.

'Watch out for them,' he told his trainees. 'They like to look important in imposing robes, and be bowed to in public. They expect the front seats in the meeting house, and the top table at dinners. They cover up what they do with long prayers, and eat the property of helpless widows. They are storing up fearful consequences for themselves when the VRIN war starts.'

Then Jesus saw how the trainees were impressed by the wealthy. They were awed as the rich gave big gifts into the Temple treasury. So when he saw a poor widow put in two small copper coins, he tackled his trainees.

'Get this straight,' he told them. 'That poor widow put in more than all of them. What all of them gave cost them nothing. She has nothing, but she's given everything.'

And then he heard his trainees say how fabulous the Temple stonework and decorations were. So he made a last attempt to open their eyes to their future.

'This Temple,' he told them, 'will soon be a pile of rubble. Not one stone will be left standing; it will all be a ruin.'

'Teacher,' they asked him, 'when will that be? What sign will we be given, when it's about to happen?'

'Don't look for signs,' Jesus replied, 'in wars, earthquakes, famines, plagues, and the like. Don't get alarmed by people seeing strange things in the sky. And don't be fooled by any signs the VRIN give you. Many would-be-rulers will claim, "It's time to strike for freedom!" Don't go running after them, or panic when you hear of revolts. Such things are bound to happen before the end comes for this city.'

'But what will happen to us?' they asked, 'if the city is destroyed.'

'They'll be beating you up,' he told them, 'long before that. They'll arrest and imprison you. They'll bring you before public meetings, Governors and rulers because of me. But don't worry how you'll defend yourselves: it will be your chance to tell your story. I will give you an ability to speak and a wisdom that will defeat all of them.

'You'll be betrayed,' he warned them, 'even by family and friends. They'll kill some of you. You'll be hated by everyone, because you follow me. But through it all, God will take care of you. If you hold firm with steadfast patience, you'll win through.'

'How will we know,' they asked, 'when the city will be destroyed?'

'You'll know,' he told them, 'when you see the Roman armies surround it. So as soon as you hear that they're coming, those in Judea must get away. Those in the city must get out as fast as they can. Anyone out in the fields mustn't go back to the city. Jerusalem will be about to suffer the consequences for everything it's done. All that *The Law* and *The Prophets* forewarned will come true.

'Heaven help those pregnant and nursing babies when it happens. They'll suffer the most, and be the cruellest victims. This whole generation will be slaughtered by the sword, or carried off as slaves to the nations. Jerusalem will be trampled on by the Romans until there's nothing left.

'As their armies flood over the land, it will seem like the end of the world. There'll be confusion and panic everywhere. Men will die of fright as their world collapses around them. They'll think the sky itself is caving in. Then everyone will know who's telling the truth. They'll see who the servant of God's power and glory really is.

'People across the earth will be stunned by this Temple's destruction. But you must be ready for it at any time. So don't let your purpose be weakened by everyday concerns, indulgence or getting drunk. Then you won't be taken by surprise and trapped in the city when the Romans arrive. Pray that you may have the strength to escape at that moment.'

'Pray too that you may persist in your loyalty to God's true servant. The Romans' approach will herald your liberation – just as buds in spring herald the summer. With this city's end its rulers will no longer be able to persecute you. I'm telling you the truth: it will happen to those of this generation. If it doesn't happen, you can forget all about me!'

Amongst the crowds by day he was safe teaching in the Temple. At dusk he slipped out of the city to the Mount of Olives for the night. And each dawn it seemed everyone in the city got up early to listen to him. The authorities were stumped. But evil was about to strike back.

12 The ruler is recognised and crowned

[22.1-23.49]

Ever since his surprise entry into the city, the chief priests had been plotting to assassinate him. Now the great day of the Festival had almost arrived – and with it the week eating Liberation bread. The authorities were getting desperate. But then they got their break.

Jesus had made a man named Judas from Kerioth one of the twelve. Judas was a southerner, and evil got the better of him. He went to the chief priests and Temple police, and offered to help them seize Jesus. They were delighted, and agreed to reward him well. So he waited for the chance to betray Jesus to them when the crowds weren't around.

Knowing what his trainees were like, Jesus told them nothing of his plans for the Liberation supper. He waited till the morning when the Liberation lambs were killed and the meal prepared. Then he called just Peter and John to him, and gave them instructions.

'Go and get the Liberation supper ready,' he said.

'Where?' they asked him.

'Listen carefully,' he replied. 'When you go into the city, a man carrying a pitcher of water will meet you. Follow him. When he goes into a house, go in after him, and give the owner this password. "The teacher says 'have you a room where I can

eat the Liberation supper with my trainees?'"
He'll show you a large upstairs room already laid
out. Prepare everything for us there.'

They went and found things exactly as he'd
told them, and got the Liberation family supper
ready. At dusk Liberation day started, and the
others were led to the house. There, Jesus took the
place of the father of the family at table. His family were his envoys, the renewed twelve tribes'
founding fathers. He gave the Liberation message,
and began:

'I've been burning to share this Liberation supper with you before I suffer the time of anguish.
But I won't eat any of this food. My Liberation
supper will be for real. It will set up God's government on earth forever.'

Then – fully aware of what was about to happen to him – he took up the first cup of wine. He
thanked God for it and handed it to them.

'Take this,' he said, 'and share it among
yourselves. I won't taste this wine again. The cup
I have to drink will plant God's government on
earth once and for all.'

Then he began to unpack the meaning of the
meal. He took the unleavened Liberation bread –
that fed those liberated by Moses – and thanked
God for it. He broke it in pieces, and gave it to
them to share round. But it now had a strange
new meaning.

'This is my body,' he said. 'It's being given for
your sake. Eat this bread to remember the liberation that I am bringing you.'

His words had changed the bread into food to feed the newly liberated people on their journey. And at the end of supper he handed them the second cup of wine. This was no longer a symbol of the lamb's blood that saved the lives of Moses' people.

'This wine,' he said, 'is the symbol of my blood. It's being shed for your sake. It seals God's promised new contract to renew the universe. But watch out! My betrayer is sharing this table with me. God's servant is on course as planned, but his betrayer is heading for destruction.'

That started them trying to work out which of them would think of doing such a thing. And that led on to an argument about who was next in line after Jesus!

'Idolatrous rulers,' Jesus broke in, 'lord it over people. They make people serve them, and then call themselves "the people's benefactor"! That's not the way you'll exercise power. Among you, the most powerful will be the one who acts as the least important. The one in command will be the person serving.'

This was an idea they just couldn't grasp, however much he drummed it into them. So Jesus tried again:

'Who's in charge, the person giving orders at the table, or the one serving him? You think it's the one at the table, don't you? Yet all I do is serve you.'

But they were set on being served, not serving, so Jesus promised them, 'I'm going to give royal power to those who've stuck with me through all my anguish. The same royal power my Father has given me. You'll eat and drink my food at my table, and share my government. You'll sit on thrones to rule the twelve tribes of God's people.'

Unable to grasp what kind of thrones he was talking about, this confirmed their wildest fantasies. But Jesus turned to Peter whom he'd nick-named Rock.

'Peter,' he said, 'Peter, watch out! Evil is right now looking for its chance to sift all of you like wheat. But I've prayed for you, Peter. I've prayed that you will be a rock, and that your loyalty won't fail. So when you decide to turn back to God, build up your brothers' loyalty.'

'Master,' a puzzled Peter replied, 'I'm ready to go to prison and death with you!'

'I'll tell you something, Peter,' Jesus said. 'The cock won't crow until you've denied three times you ever knew me.'

Peter wanted to protest, but Jesus turned to them all:

'When I sent you out without a purse, bag, or sandals, were you short of anything?'

'No,' they said, 'not a thing.'

'Well now,' he told them, 'everything has changed. As you go out to proclaim God's sovereignty, take your money and bag. And anyone who hasn't got a sword will need to sell his cloak and buy one. It's now certain that the scripture is about to be fulfilled by me:

He was convicted as a rebel.

In fact, everything written in *The Law* and *The Prophets* about me is coming true.'

'Look master,' they said, 'we've already got two swords.'

Jesus just gave up. There was no way he could get through to them.

'You just aren't getting it,' he said.

Then he left the house and went, as he'd been doing each night, to the Mount of Olives. His trainees followed behind, and when he reached his chosen spot, he turned to them.

'Pray,' he told them. 'Pray that you won't have to suffer the time of terrible anguish.'

Then he took himself away from them about a stone's throw. There he knelt down, and his great battle with evil began.

'Father,' he prayed, 'please, please, save me from having to go through with this. But let me follow your plan to the finish, and not mine.'

He was in agony, and it seemed one of God's messengers appeared to strengthen his resolve. He prayed so passionately, that his sweat became drops of blood spattering the ground.

When he got up from praying, he came back to his trainees. He found them fast asleep, exhausted by their distress at the state he was in.

'What are you doing sleeping?' he said. 'Get up! Pray that you don't have to suffer the terrible anguish.'

Even as he was saying it a crowd appeared out of the darkness. One of them came towards Jesus to own him as his master with a kiss. They saw it was Judas from Kerioth.

'Judas,' Jesus asked him, 'are you going to betray me with a kiss of loyalty?'

Then the trainees now woke up to what was happening.

'Master,' they said, 'shall we use our swords?' And one of them slashed at the High Priest's servant, cutting off his right ear.

'Hold it! Enough of that!' Jesus ordered, touching the man's ear and healing him. Even the man arresting him was welcome to a share in the new age.

Jesus addressed the priestly officers, Temple guard commanders and lords who'd come to arrest him. 'Anyone would think I'm a rebel,' he said. 'Why have you come with swords and clubs to arrest me? Every day I've been with you in the Temple, and you never raised a finger against me. But you choose to act when darkness rules.'

They grabbed hold of him, and led him off back into the city. His trainees made their escape, but Peter followed the party at a distance. They took Jesus into the courtyard of the High Priest's palace. A fire had been lit in the middle of the courtyard, and Peter joined people round it.

A servant-girl saw Peter sitting in the firelight, and stared hard at him. 'This man was with him,' she said.

No way did Peter want to get arrested too. He was there to get Jesus released. 'I don't know him, woman,' Peter said, denying any knowledge of Jesus.

But shortly afterwards someone else noticed him. 'You're one of them,' he said.

'Not me, mate,' Peter said.

And then about an hour later another man kept on pointing to him.

'I'm sure he was with him,' the man insisted. 'You can tell he's a northerner.'

'Look man,' Peter said, 'I just don't know what you're talking about.'

And as he was saying it the cock crowed. The Master turned and looked directly at Peter. The words, 'denied three times you ever knew me,' broke Peter down. He went straight out into the street, and wept agonised tears.

The men holding Jesus began to make fun of him and knock him about. They blindfolded him, and kept punching him.

'If you're a prophet,' they taunted, 'prophesy who's going to hit you next.'

All through the night they kept pouring out a stream of abuse at him. Then at day break the lords, chief priests and legal authorities met. They brought Jesus into their Council chamber to be tried before them, and began, 'If you're the ruler, just tell us.'

'But if I do, you won't believe me,' Jesus replied. 'And when I put the question to you, you refuse to answer it. This is the time *The Law* and *The Prophets* foretold. God is giving his servant sovereignty on earth forever.'

'Ah, you are the ruler!' they all chimed out.

'You say that I am the ruler,' he answered.

'Why do we need any more evidence?' they said. 'Hasn't he admitted it?'

With that they jumped up, and took Jesus over to the Roman Governor, Pilate. But their relations with Pilate were fraught. The stubborn, boorish Governor couldn't conceal his contempt for them. So the whole Council went *en masse*. And to impress Pilate with the seriousness of the case, they began a long list of accusations.

'We caught this man,' they charged, 'leading the whole nation astray. He forbids us to pay taxes to the Emperor. He claims that he's God's promised ruler of the Jews...'

'Well, well,' Pilate broke in, quietly mocking the Council. Any less likely ruler than this beaten-up figure in front of him was hard to imagine. How fitting of Jews to think him a ruler!

'You,' he said turning to Jesus, 'are the ruler of the Jews!'

Like the Council, the Governor too had now affirmed Jesus the promised ruler! His words made Jesus the Emperor's overlord – as the prophets foretold.

'Those are your words,' Jesus answered.

It was clear to Pilate the prisoner wasn't a rebel. The charges were bogus, and an attempt to drag the Governor into their Jewish infighting. It seemed a good chance to put them in their place.

'I find no reason to convict this man,' Pilate announced at once.

The Jewish authorities erupted.

'But his teaching is stirring people up throughout all Judea,' they clamoured. 'He caused trouble up in the north and he's doing the same here.'

When they said 'the north', Pilate asked if he was a northerner. And when they said yes, that made him Herod's subject. Since Herod was in Jerusalem for the Festival, Pilate ordered them to take Jesus over to Herod.

When Herod saw Jesus being brought in, he was gleeful. He'd wanted to interrogate him for a long time, because of the signs Jesus was giving. He was hoping to see Jesus perform one, and spent a long time questioning him. But Jesus wouldn't say anything to him.

The chief priests and the legal experts stood there, pouring out accusations. In the end Herod had to give up, and resorted to mocking him. Since he was charged with being ruler he ordered his soldiers to bow to Jesus. Then Herod himself joined in bowing with them. After that he dressed Jesus in stately robes, and sent him back to Pilate.

The result of this exchange was ironic. Jesus' policy was to turn Jews and Romans from enemies into friends. Until now Pilate and Herod had been sworn enemies. Herod's act in returning Jesus to Pilate changed all that. The same day these two, Jew and Roman, became friends.

It was ironic too that all the terms for the ruler of the Jews were now met. Jesus had been owned by the people, the High Priest, the puppet-ruler, and the Empire itself! And because Herod had sent Jesus back, Pilate summoned the chief priests, lords and their people again.

'You brought this man to me,' he told them, 'charging him with leading the people astray. I've examined him in your presence, and have found the man not guilty. So has Herod, because he's sent him back to us. It's clear that the man is innocent of the charges you brought against him. He's done nothing to deserve death, so I'm going to have him flogged and let him go.'

At the festival it was a custom for the Governor to release a prisoner. But his decision to release Jesus brought a furious reaction.

'Get rid of him!' shouted the crowd, and started to chant, 'We want Barabbas!'

Barabbas was leader of an attempted uprising that had just taken place. He was awaiting crucifixion for murder, and was the sort of leader people understood. They wanted someone who'd pay the Romans back what they deserved.

Pilate tried telling them again that it was his intention to let Jesus go. But they wouldn't give up.

'Crucify him!' they howled, 'Crucify him!'

Then Pilate tried for a third time.

'Why?' he asked them, 'What has he done? I can't find anything he's done that deserves death. I'll have him flogged, and let him go.'

But the yelling of 'Crucify him!' grew louder all the time. Pilate began to get worried, and decided to give them what they wanted. He freed the violent revolutionary, Barabbas, the man they asked for. Then he handed the man of peace, Jesus, to be dealt with as they wished.

When the soldiers had finished with him, Jesus was too weak to carry his cross. So as they led him out to crucifixion, they grabbed a man named Simon. Simon was just arriving at the city that moment from the North African port of Cyrene. They made him pick up the cross, and carry it behind Jesus.

A great crowd of people followed, among them women, wailing in mourning for him. Jesus turned to them.

'Women of Jerusalem,' he said, 'don't cry for me. Weep for your own fate and that of your children. If they do this to an innocent man, what will happen to the guilty? Your fate will be unbearable:

> The lucky ones will be the barren wombs that never bore children, the women with breasts that never nursed them.
>
> For your destruction and exile in foreign lands is certain.

Two revolutionaries were led out to be tortured to death with him. When they reached the place called The Skull, they crucified Jesus there. They hung the two revolutionaries on each side of him.

'Father, forgive them,' Jesus prayed, as they nailed him to the cross. 'They don't know what they're doing.'

Evil's last attempt to make him hate had failed. Its power was finally broken. The board, fixed above Jesus' head, proclaimed:

THIS IS THE RULER OF THE JEWS

The soldiers divided his clothes by casting lots, while the crowd stood gawking at it all. Then the Jewish authorities, who'd come to watch, started the crowd off:

'They say he freed others,' they jeered. 'If he's the ruler sent to free us, let's see him free himself!'

The soldiers too joined in the mockery with them.

'Yes, if you're the ruler of the Jews,' the soldiers taunted, 'set yourself free.' And they went up to him and offered him cheap wine.

Even one of the rebels, hanging there with him, joined in the mockery.

'Aren't you the promised ruler of the Jews?' the man said. 'Then free yourself and us!'

But the other revolutionary rebuked him.

Haven't you got any fear of God?' he said. 'You've got the same sentence as him, and we deserve it for what we did. But this man's done nothing wrong.'

Then the man added, 'Jesus, remember me when you set up your government.'

'I promise you,' Jesus replied, 'today you'll be with me in Paradise.'

By this time it was about midday, and for three hours darkness ruled the land. The sun was gone, the Temple's destruction was sealed, and Jesus died with a great shout:

'Father, I entrust my spirit into your hands.'

The centurion in charge, who had witnessed all that happened, was in awe.

'I'm sure this man was innocent,' he said. 'For sure he's been proved right in God's eyes.'

When the crowds, there for the spectacle, saw what happened, they slunk off. They went home full of remorse. His trainees – keeping well clear of the soldiers – watched everything from a distance. But the soldiers didn't bother about the women. His women followers were standing throughout as close as they wanted.

Then something unexpected happened.

13 The future has arrived...

[23.50 – 24.53]

A member of the ruling Council named Joseph from Arimathea arrived. He was a good, honest man, who wanted God's government, and hadn't agreed with the Council's decision. He had asked Pilate for Jesus' body, and Pilate had granted it to him. Joseph took Jesus' body down from the cross, and wrapped it in a shroud. He placed it in a new, unused tomb, hollowed out of rock. Then he sealed it with a round stone.

The women, who had come down from the north with Jesus, followed behind the burial group. They saw where the body was placed in the tomb, but it was already late Friday afternoon. At sunset the holy day would begin, so they went back to prepare spices and ointments. When the holy day began they stopped work to obey the commandment, and rested.

On the first day of the week, the women took spices to anoint the body. Very early that morning Mary Magdalene, Joanna, James's mother Mary and other women went to the tomb. When they arrived they found the stone placed at the entrance to the tomb rolled away. They went straight in, only to find that Jesus' body had gone.

As they stood there in shock, they suddenly found two men standing beside them. The men were dressed as if for a party, and the women were terrified. The women bowed low, unaware it was 'the first day of the week' – of a new creation!

'Why are you looking for the living among the dead?' the men asked them. 'He's not here, he's been resurrected. Don't you remember what he told you up in the north? He said that the ruler would be handed over to the Romans and crucified. Then on the third day he'd rise again.'

This brought it back to them, and they remembered what Jesus had said. Shaken and trembling, they returned from the tomb to tell the envoys. But the men didn't believe them, because the words made no sense. No one would be raised from the dead until the country was liberated. Then *all* those worthy, not just one man, would be raised.

Peter was first to get up and run to the tomb, to see what had happened. He bent down, looked into the tomb, and saw only the linen cloths lying there. He left the tomb baffled, trying to work out what could have happened.

By afternoon the Cleopases, who'd been followers of Jesus, decided to go back home. They lived about seven miles from Jerusalem, and were wrapped in discussion as they went. They were going over everything and arguing about it, when a man caught up with them. He walked along with them – yet something stopped them recognizing him.

'What's the issue,' he asked, 'that's causing you such a problem on your journey?'

They were amazed at the question. They stood there looking a picture of misery.

'You must be the only person in Jerusalem, who doesn't know what's happened there,' Cleopas said.

'What's that?' the man asked.

'To Jesus of Nazareth!' they chimed in together.

'He was the great prophet,' Cleopas exclaimed. 'He acted and spoke with power before God and all the people. But our chief priests and lords handed him over for execution, and they crucified him. We were expecting him to liberate us from the Romans.'

'Now it's the third day since all this happened,' his wife Mary said.

'And this morning,' Cleopas went on, 'some women of our group capped it all. They went to the tomb very early, and found his body had gone. They came back saying they'd seen strange messengers, who'd claimed he was alive. Some of our men went to the tomb, and they found things as the women had said. But they didn't see him.'

'How can you be so stupid?' the stranger responded. 'Don't you believe what the books of *The Law* and *The Prophets* say? Didn't the ruler have to suffer all this to reveal his authority?'

Then starting at the first book, he explained all the passages about the ruler. And when they came to their village, he made as if to go on. But they pressed him to stay with them.

'You must stay the night,' they said, 'because the sun's already set.'

So he went in to stay with them. When they sat down to eat, he took the bread, blessed it, and broke it. As he gave it to them they looked at him, and the haze lifted from their eyes. They recognised who he was – but the next moment he was no longer to be seen.

They blinked open-mouthed, and looked at each other.

'Weren't our hearts on fire,' Cleopas gasped, 'as he talked to us on the road? Now we know what *The Law* and *The Prophets* meant.'

They jumped up, and set off back to Jerusalem as fast as they could go. When they arrived, they found the eleven and those with them all gathered together.

'It's true!' they were saying. 'The Master really has been raised. He's appeared to Peter.'

Then the two of them told what had happened on the road. They said they'd recognised him when he broke the bread. And as they were saying this, Jesus himself was standing there, in the middle of them.

'Greetings, everyone,' he said.

Everyone froze on the spot. They thought they were seeing a ghost.

'Why are you shaking?' he asked them. 'Why do you doubt that it's me? Look at my hands and my feet. Can't you see it's me? Get hold of me if you want to, and see for yourself. Ghosts aren't made of flesh and bones like I am!'

As he said this, he held out his hands and feet. Yet for sheer joy they couldn't believe what they were seeing. They were dumb-struck, and couldn't believe what was happening.

'Have you got anything to eat?' he asked them.

They handed him a piece of cooked fish. He took it, and ate it before their eyes, but still they couldn't be fully convinced.

'While I was with you,' he said, 'I told you what would happen. The whole story written about me in *The Law and The Prophets* had to be completed.'

And as he unpacked the story, their blocked minds began to clear.

'The prophets foretold that the ruler would give his life to free his people,' he said. 'The prophets declared that on the third day he would rise from the dead. Then, starting from Jerusalem, the great news of the ruler's victory would be proclaimed to every nation.

'So the nations no longer need to be slaves, serving man-made gods. All are now freed to accept God's forgiveness of their sins. You are the witnesses of these things. And as my Father promised through the prophets I will equip you for the new age. Stay here in the city, until you're clothed with the power of the Spirit.'

The truth was slowly seeping into their battered brains. The establishment had condemned Jesus as a false ruler. But God had resurrected him: therefore he was the promised ruler, and the cross was his victory! Evil at its worst had recoiled on evil itself. Jesus had overcome evil – the enemy – by showing true humanity. Where every other human had failed, he had proved victorious. The whole world could see it.

Jesus' last act was to lead his trainees out of the city as far as Bethany. Then he raised his hands to bless them, and parted from them into God's dimension. The job was done. He was enthroned, as the prophet had declared – in everlasting authority and power over all nations.

His appointed heralds returned to Jerusalem powered by joy. They spent their time in the Temple, praising God for the wonder of his ways. Their task was now to broadcast the great news from the rooftops. Unheard of and startling events were about to explode upon the world.

Postscript

14 ...and *The Law* was tragically fulfilled

The whole world now knows what happened to those who followed the VRIN. There's no need for an account here. As Jesus foretold, their idolatry brought its horrific consequences. The VRIN first murdered the Jewish rulers, then each other, and ended in all-out war with Rome.

The Romans first stormed the towns of the north. Any VRIN who escaped fled to Jerusalem. When the Romans at last surrounded the city, it was Festival time. Three would-be-rulers were fighting in the city to rule there, and horrors unspeakable were committed. No other city ever endured such suffering. The VRIN showed their inhumanity to the world.

Roman siege engines brought buildings crashing down, burying those inside. Then the Romans broke through the walls. Those they didn't kill they sold as slaves among the nations. When no victims or plunder were left, they razed the city and Temple to the ground.

But it is to the next part of Jesus' unique story that I must turn – the story of how his heralds proclaimed the real news to Rome itself.

Glossary

Word definitions can depend on who's using them...

VRIN reads as		Jesus reads as
the time when true Jews will rule the land	**age to come**	the time when God rules the people
code for liberation from Rome	**desert**	code for liberation from evil
God's name when the Jews are liberated	**Father**	God's name when people are freed from evil
time of God's return when Jews are liberated	**forgiveness of sins**	God has forgiven and is returning
the territory of Israel	**the land**	becoming the whole earth
i. celebrates the liberation by Moses ii. the coming liberation from Rome	**Liberation Festival**	i. celebrates the liberation by Moses ii. the decisive coming liberation from evil
i. Jews an independent nation state ii. Jewish martyrs bodily risen into it	**resurrection**	i. people restored as full Jews ii. bodily risen from the dead
serving idols, (mostly by their ancestors)	**sin, sinners**	all those guilty of serving idols

i. the Jewish people and	son-of-God	i. those obedient to God
ii. a title of the Jewish ruler		ii. a title of the promised ruler
the ruler to liberate them from Rome	son-of-David	the promised ruler, liberator from evil
the true Jews	VRIN	Jews who make idols of land, race, the Temple and custom

Endnotes

1   Luke 21:27, 21:26, 14:26, 18:22, 16:8

2   Luke 8.10

3   Luke 8.8

4   Mark 8 18

Lightning Source UK Ltd.
Milton Keynes UK
15 December 2010
164418UK00001B/15/P